THE MUSIC OF THE

The Music of The Other
New Challenges for Ethnomusicology in a Global Age

LAURENT AUBERT

With a Foreword by
ANTHONY SEEGER

Translated by
CARLA RIBEIRO

ASHGATE

Published by
Ashgate Publishing Limited
Wey Court East
Union Road
Farnham
Surrey GU9 7PT
England

Ashgate Publishing Company
Suite 420
101 Cherry Street
Burlington, VT 05401-4405
USA

Reprinted 2009

Ashgate website: http://www.ashgate.com

British Library Cataloguing in Publication Data
Aubert, Laurent
   The music of the other : new challenges for ethnomusicology in a global age
   1.Ethnomusicology
   I.Title
   780.8'9

Library of Congress Cataloging-in-Publication Data
Aubert, Laurent.
   [Musique de l'autre. English]
   The music of the other : new challenges for ethnomusicology in a global age / Laurent Aubert ; translated by Carla Ribeiro.
      p. cm. Includes bibliographical references (p.   ).
   1. Ethnomusicology. I. Title.
ML3798.A8313 2007
   780.89–dc22

                                                                              2006016795

ISBN 978-0-7546-5343-1 (pbk)

Printed and bound in Great Britain by TJ International Ltd, Padstow, Cornwall

Mixed Sources
Product group from well-managed forests and other controlled sources
www.fsc.org Cert no. SGS-COC-2482
FSC © 1996 Forest Stewardship Council

Printed and bound in Great Britain by
TJ International Ltd, Padstow, Cornwall.

Contents

Foreword

Anthony Seeger

One day in early summer 2003 I spent a delightful afternoon in intense conversation with a colleague during a break in the annual meeting of the French Society for Ethnomusicology. Sitting in a small café on the shore of the Mediterranean, drinking excellent coffee and eating local food, we talked about music. Our conversation ranged widely over issues of representation in concerts, the publishing of compact discs and the complex roles those who study or document the musical traditions of the world play in the perception of music today. We had not had an earlier opportunity to talk, and on this memorable afternoon I discovered Laurent Aubert to be a quiet, urbane, thoughtful and very experienced observer of the world of music. At the time I was unfamiliar with his 2001 publication, which you have in your hand in English translation. Reading this book you can have a similar experience to my own, although you must find your own café. This book allows you to encounter an original mind, one who brings his experience and wide reading to ask very important questions about music today and to offer very thoughtful, frequently subtle and multi-faceted, responses to them.

Music and food are two features of human culture that circulate most widely in the world today while maintaining elements of their origins. Gastronomic diversity is largely the result of population movements and displacements. Musical diversity, on the other hand, is influenced much more by a global industry devoted to selling products, filling concert halls, making money and (in the case of ethnomusicology) studying, teaching and disseminating knowledge. Although part of the significance of 'ethnic' food is an exposure to new tastes, in most cases local preferences and expectations shape the food that is offered by restaurants or available in the frozen food section of supermarkets. In the same way, the interest in 'world music' today is driven by a fascination with musical difference, but often requires musicians to adapt their sounds to fit what the new audiences are able to or interesting in hearing, to adjust to the demands of the proscenium stage and the audience's sleeping and working hours, and to provide themselves and the larger industry with an income.

Ethnomusicologists – specialists in the study and often the presentation of music from different parts of the world – were among the first to pay close and serious attention to the musical traditions of distant places. Like authors whose travelogues would describe the food delicacies of distant cultures, for decades the publications of ethnomusicologists provided tantalising hints of unexpected sounds. Ethnomusicologists were helped, to some degree, by a recording technology that allowed them to present truncated and often low-fidelity representations of what they described on wax cylinders and on 78- and 33⅓-rpm discs. From the beginning of the twentieth century they released 'ethnic' recordings that were heard by at most a few thousand scholars and enthusiasts. This comfortable situation changed dramatically in the 1970s with the enthusiasm of a large number of non-ethnomusicologists for the non-European sounds suddenly available to them not only on recordings but also in festivals and concert halls. Suddenly ethnomusicologists were no longer controlling the dissemination of world music: they were engulfed in a flood of it produced by others. The new cicerones were often popular musicians in their own right – Yehudi Menuhin introduced Ravi Shankar to Carnegie Hall; Paul Simon's album, *Graceland*, brought Ladysmith Black Mambazo to many millions of amazed listeners; and the record labels of Peter Gabriel, Mickey Hart and others enabled many of their own fans to become adepts of the lesser-known music they released. Laurent Aubert's book engages the reader with the many challenges the sudden popularity of 'world music' presents to ethnomusicologists, to musicians and to audiences in Europe and the United States. He ponders the dangers as well as the benefits for all parties of this sudden popularity, and he draws on his own experience as a student and performer of one of the musical traditions of India, and as an author, a publisher and a wide-ranging reader.

Just as the music native to different parts of the world uses different timbres and offers new musical experiences, so the academic disciplines of different countries focus on different aspects of their objects of investigation. One of the reasons this book is so important to English-speaking audiences is that an significant part of its bibliography will be unknown to them. France has played a key role in the popularization of the musical traditions of other parts of the world for at least 150 years, and French thinkers have reflected on what Aubert calls 'a game of mirrors' through which each perceives the other for just as long. He draws on insightful comments by Victor Segalen in 1911, builds some of his thinking on the work of the anthropologist Louis Dumont and the ethnomusicologist John Blacking, and presents examples from Paris.

One of the reasons reading this book reminded me so much of our afternoon in southern France is that the author has drawn together a number of his publications from different sources and different times. The result, however, is not a collection of separate essays but rather a delightful exploration of diverse but related topics as one might undertake in a prolonged conversation with a friend. The book does not pretend to be exhaustive or to define all of its terms precisely; but it is at different moments provocative, passionate, sympathetic and self-reflective. Each chapter will certainly generate further debate and discussion. This makes it ideal for ethnomusicology courses, of course, but also makes for very stimulating reading.

This slim volume is an important reflection on the impact of the popularization of the musical traditions of the world on (among others) musicians, producers and scholars. All of these will benefit from reading the ideas herein.

Anthony Seeger
September 2005

Translator's Note

Aubert's writing probes and ponders, illustrating points in rather imagistic style and flowing swiftly without the conventional reiterations of an academic textbook. He selects his words carefully, colourfully, sometimes for the provocatively jarring effect that particular combinations have on our everyday assumptions. And he's not afraid to be vocal and discursive, directly addressing the reader with questions and qualifications that run on directly from the experiences described. I have striven as far as possible to retain Aubert's animated and conversational style in this translation. I am grateful to Laurent Aubert for reviewing the entire book in translation, and to Jonathan Stock both for initially suggesting the project and then for editing the final English – any errors that remain, therefore, are entirely his!

Carla Ribeiro

Preface

The great flood into our most immediate cultural environment of music of the world and of its agents is a relatively recent phenomenon. This new order, now well on the way to completely transforming all our musical standards, is nothing but a consequence of the vast process of globalisation characterising the contemporary age. It is linked particularly to the exponential acceleration of the flow of migrants, to the growth of the tourist trade and to the development of communication technologies, the consequences of which are progressively affecting all arenas of the human conscience. This observation has led me to become interested in the place now occupied in our experience by music from elsewhere; to consider the influence this music exercises on our values, our habits and our cultural practices; and, conversely, to try to evaluate the impact of this situation, both on our perception of the other and on the future of this music and of its practitioners.

The texts united in this volume were for the most part already published elsewhere: in journals, collective works and in the acts of colloquia. They appear here in revised form and newly shaped, intended to give the set maximum coherence, to update certain passages and to cut repetitions. The wish to regroup them was born from the fact that they all set out from a shared perspective. Namely each approaches a particular aspect with the aim of widening the field of ethnomusicology by situating debate in an area not generally tackled by specialists: that of our own society, a society already multi-ethnic and multicultural, one that each day resembles more closely the global village spoken of by Marshall McLuhan as far back as 1970.

These issues are still relatively rarely approached by ethnomusicologists, who prefer – and no one is blaming them – to concentrate their research on a given musical tradition, studying all its parameters, including possible urban developments and transnational extensions. This approach is without doubt indispensable; it is even at the base of the discipline, and it is true that immersion in another musical culture is the only means to grasp its mechanisms, to understand its structures and to find out its principles and identifying criteria. From one point of view it also has value as an initiatory path, insofar as personal involvement is necessarily a leading part of this approach; consciously or not, the quest for the other in its difference is always also a quest for oneself by way of the other.

In the broadest way, ethnomusicological research has contributed to the supply of data from which it should be possible to establish a veritable musical map of humanity and, thus, to develop an anthropological approach to all types of music, including our own. In this regard, I subscribe completely to the remarks of John Blacking when he wrote: 'Ethnomusicology has the power to create a revolution in the world of music and music education, if it follows the implications of its discoveries and develops as a method, and not merely an area, of study' (1973: 4).

Blacking thus laid the foundation of a genuine anthropology of music in which people as music-makers must be at the centre of the debate, whatever the cultural context in which their activity occurs. In principle, this perspective appears only to point out the most obvious common sense; but, in integrating all music, including the Western art music tradition, it implies fundamentally that 'classical' and historical musicology can no longer be considered anything more than a particular application of this broader musicology in its own specific domain, no more the norm of everything in the matter of musicality – this, of course, has generated some resistance.

If ethnomusicologists have contributed to opening the gates of our perception to 'music of the world' in its great diversity, they on the other hand never imagined the passion that certain types of music would be able to arouse among the public at large. And yet, often independent of the efforts of specialists, these diverse musical genres have become widely accessible, coming to us in the form of concerts, discs, radio and television broadcasts, or seen on dedicated Internet sites. Or else we seek them out ourselves on location by means of journeys of enthusiasm dedicated to penetrating their mystery or in simple curiosity aided by the facilities offered by the development of cultural tourism.

This enlargement of our artistic horizons has turned out to be extremely stimulating: acting like a catalyst, it has brought into question numerous preconceptions about other cultures of the world; it has opened our experience to different ways of pondering over, producing and perceiving music; it has contributed to enlivening a whole sector of contemporary creation, from the serious to the popular, by bringing in new dimensions, previously unknown techniques, and conceptions of space and time very often radically distinct from our own. Finally, it has opened the doors of the music industry to expressions that have traditionally had no such access and the subsequent flood, linked to the massive migrations that characterise our time, has given birth to the concept of world music and to its commercial exploitation.

As a symbolic form, music is a manner of apprehending the world and acting on it. A general assessment of the impact of globalisation on music still remains to be written, but this book may perhaps contribute to the widening of that debate, suggesting to music lovers a few lines of reflection on a major cultural phenomenon. Our discovery of the music of the other is an experience, a transcultural experience from one person to another in which the perception of the other in his or her difference mingles intimately with that of our own sensitivity vis-à-vis the other. This ability to listen also contributes to transforming its object while imposing new stakes. In addition it brings us to consider such notions as universality and otherness from a new angle: indeed if, as one hears, music is a universal language, of what music do we speak, wherein lies its universality and under which conditions does it emerge?

Chapter 1

The Elsewhere of Music
Paradoxes of a Multicultural Society

Identity in Question

If music has its own place in all reflections on culture, it does so in my opinion by the stakes it represents. Music is indeed never insignificant. It is simultaneously a strong and unifying means of communication and a revealer of identity within the abundance of models that characterise our society. We identify ourselves with music that we like because it corresponds to our sensibility and vision of the world; we draw apart from other music when it is foreign to our affinities and fail to 'speak' to us. Through its content music is always a bearer of meanings. If Plato could write that 'the music and literature of a country cannot be altered without major political and social changes' (1974: 191) that is because the music he is referring to was at the same time the echo and model of something other than itself. Furthermore, it was endowed of powers susceptible to affect the whole bundle of realities, as much physiological as political and cultural.

One of the main aims of ethnomusicology is to approach these relations between music and society, to consider the complex networks of interdependence existing in any social entity between, on one hand, the context and circumstances of a musical act – collective or individual – and, on the other, the nature and modalities of the act itself. Thus, musical and social structures coexist in a relation of close solidarity, and every reflection on the significance or the aesthetics of music will necessarily send us back to the study of mentalities. A musical fact does not define itself only by its acoustic components and the technical means by which these are produced, but equally by its substance and by what it implies, by our grasping of a coherent set of criteria, a social and spiritual function, an attested psychological and possibly ritual efficacy, the role traditionally assigned to its producers and receivers, and, finally, the appropriate methods of learning and diffusion.

In this conception of music, Plato deliberately disregards the role of the individual in the process of musical creation. He tends to reduce music to its social role, assimilating its work or production to a merely utilitarian, social, ritual and symbolic function. This form of reductionism, which is to say the negation of the autonomy of the individual, seems to predominate in numerous traditional societies and is opposed to the modern ideology of art, which is fundamentally individualistic and libertarian.[1] In this respect, the process of globalisation causes a kind of 'reciprocal

---

1   'As opposed to modern society, traditional societies, which know nothing of equality and liberty as values, which know nothing, in short, of the individual, have basically a

exoticism shock' through the imposed confrontation of these two universes and the new perception that each develops of the other. If one believes Victor Segalen (1995: 25): 'Exoticism is therefore not an adaptation; it is not the perfect understanding of oneself that one would embrace in itself, but the sharp and immediate perception of an eternal incomprehension.'

Perspectives opened up in the wide market for world music have an impact on the evolution of this music, leading it into a confrontation with new challenges. Does the rise of migratory movements and communicative freeways place in question principles of everyone's identity in the name of integration? Or is this integration the major opportunity of our time, one which will allow us all to reach a more just and tolerant, humanistic perception of each other? Obviously, this question does not concern music alone; it could apply to practically all the other domains of human activity, whether politics, religion, art, handicraft or even cuisine or sexual practices. Does the multiplicity of present models contribute to self-enrichment, or does it rather generate a simple juxtaposition of ethnic or ideological ghettos without bridges to some by way of the others?

The question of identity is placed simultaneously on the collective level (with 'objective' components such as adherence to a civilisation, religion, community, ethnicity, social class, age, political party and so on) and on the individual level (with 'subjective' components – how individuals situate themselves in relation to these components). Far from being insignificant, the problematic of identity is perhaps one of the most challenging that we must face; it is at the source of schisms and the most serious conflicts generated by the present postcolonial period. The remarkable work of Amin Maalouf, *On identity* (*Les identities meurtrières*), pinpoints the problem with rare acuity (2000: 30):

> In the age of globalisation and of the ever-accelerating intermingling of elements in which we are all caught up, a new concept of identity is needed, and needed urgently. We cannot be satisfied with forcing billions of bewildered human beings to choose between excessive assertion of their identity and the loss of the identity altogether, between fundamentalism and disintegration. But that is the logical consequence of the prevailing attitude on the subject. If our contemporaries are not encouraged to accept their multiple affiliations and allegiances; if they cannot reconcile their need for identity with an open and unprejudiced tolerance of other cultures; if they feel they have to choose between denial of the self and denial of the other – then we shall be bringing into being legions of the lost and hordes of the bloodthirsty madmen.

Even if the risks incurred are not of the same kind, the case of musical identity is nevertheless exemplary. The reason for this is that all music is a bearer of a set of values, at the same time ethical (by use of a set of references to which it appeals and expresses according to appropriate means) and aesthetic (through codes put to work and their effects on the senses and the psyche). As a means of expression, musical

---

collective idea of man, and our (residual) apperception of man as a social being is the sole link which unites us to them, and is the only angle from we can come to understand them' (Dumont 1980: 8).

identity acts to reveal notions beyond those of the field of musical production and consumption.

The question of musical identity is evidently not always put so sharply. For example, it has practically no raison d'être in so-called 'archaic' societies, or even in the past of civilisations with a more varied social fabric, including our own. The role of every musical category was clearly determined, and its use the object of relative consensus within a community. Music constituted a resonant representation of social structures, and the full array of its demonstrations expressed the consistency of a civilisation as a functioning unit and of its principles. It goes without saying that in such a society the field of music was likely to contain internal contradictions.

The field of music is practically unlimited in the contemporary world. Consciously or not our individual choices are established according to education, sensitivity and a whole body of affinities, among them artistic, social, political and ideological. The individual choices made demonstrate a person's position, sometimes even in opposition to the ways and conventions of the social group to which he or she belongs. Thus, a taste for baroque music, rap or techno is not neutral: to a certain extent in every case it implies an adherence to the vision of the world displayed by one or another of these genres. Is it then necessary to unravel, as Sartre remarks, 'the pragmatic truth [which] has replaced the revealed truth'? In this respect, Jean During (1994a: 27) points out that in music in the modern world, as in all the arts, one of the most significant features, if not the most evident, is the replacement of the concept of Beauty, which is subjected to a concept of Truth, by the concept of taste, which lies in the domain of contingency and individual subjectivity.

The Local and the Global

It is no secret that the proliferation of modern Western civilisation and its ideals all over the world has provoked deep and irreversible distresses whose consequences have affected each and every domain of culture. Clearly the colonial age established the premises for this; but, paradoxically, colonial power remained on the whole rather indifferent to matters of art and culture. One might say that it was as if colonialisation limited itself to the planet's political conquest, to the seizure of its economic wealth and commercial networks and, more incidentally, to Christianisation. In fact, it was the old colonies' declarations of independence and the formation of nation states that, essentially for economic reasons, accelerated and disseminated the various processes of de-culturation. Today, crystallised and inevitable political and social tensions in numerous regions of the world ensue directly from these circumstances, and, as a direct consequence, we see the consolidation of existing antagonisms opposing 'fundamentalists', 'revivalists' and 'progressivists'.

Given the scale of this crisis, its musical repercussions can appear anecdotal. They are nevertheless informative of the movement in which they play a part. Indeed, rare are the cases where the introduction of modern production tools had no impact on the foundations of a culture's traditional thought and its artistic expressions, and therefore of its music. In extreme cases nothing but the most recent developments remain today from millennial traditions. They are subject to different pressures

– ideological and economic – imposed by the contemporary environment, or subsequently by the touristic, commercial or political usages of official, 'sweetened' folklore revivals.

Every alteration of music's role and context inevitably implies a structural and semantic displacement of its manifestations. Certainly, musical forms have always evolved during their history, whatever the time or scale in which one considers the process. At all times, migrations of peoples have permitted a confrontation of knowledge and techniques which has contributed to the widening of the field of individual experience, often causing regenerative cross-breeding. Musicians met, exchanged experiences, techniques, repertoires and instruments, contributing through their capacity for absorption and synthesis to the broadening and renewal of their musical idiom. Nevertheless, the generalisation all over the planet of the cultural hybridisation process observed today is a phenomenon without precedent.

Whereas historic intertwinings and syncretisms result in a way from 'natural' factors, linked to migrations – voluntary or forced – and to the consequential meeting of cultures, hybridisation distinguishes itself above all by its experimental, voluntary and utilitarian aspects. It inevitably introduces a relation of power between the existing parts because of their respective inequality. Back in 1976, the Vietnamese musicologist Tran Van Khê revealed that the application of hybridisation has the tendency to provoke the deterioration of the 'musical body', which is often the weakest component of the symbiosis with regard to its resistance and adaptability. On this subject, he noted in particular a kind of '… enrichment when borrowed elements are compatible with the original tradition and impoverishment in the contrary case. In sum, it is a problem of compatibility or incompatibility between the existing elements, just as in the case of successful graft or biologic rejection' (1976: 8).[2]

The most eminent and widespread example of musical hybridity is the variety of national or international music that is progressively under way, spilling out and saturating the resonant environment of the world's cities and countries. Systematically disseminated by the media, it tends to become universally the new norm, insofar as it is nearly the only music whose propagation reaches all layers of the population, crossing comfortably political, social and linguistic borders. Everywhere is the same: the 'preparation' process involves an intellectual dose of traditional significations, the manipulation of mentalities, fashion movements and associated technologies. It aims to reinforce a frame of mind that is compliant to modern tastes, 'politically correct' and devoid of all subversive desire. Hence, it diverts the public from its autonomy, and in a large measure from its legitimate preoccupations, and towards a diet of easily accessible, easily consumed products.

One of the extreme forms of this tendency is so-called 'ambient music'. It is distilled throughout the day by loudspeakers in supermarkets, waiting rooms and public places of all kinds. Destined to 'furnish the silence', this supposedly 'light'

---

2   Marc Augé has written on this subject that 'All deficiencies in the identity/otherness pair correspond to a weakening that we witness when situations of "cultural contact" such as colonization or modernization shake up the internal structures of local cosmologics' (1998: 30).

music is, nevertheless, not created to be as insignificant as it appears to be. Some specialised producers have studied the mechanisms of conscience penetration. They have done so scientifically from research advances in acoustics, marketing, statistics and in the psychology of the masses. Without expanding a great deal on the topic, let us note that this type of insidious resonant environment is envisaged and achieved via the following precise goals: to generate passivity, bait the customer, create a dream to anaesthetise pain or hunt down problems, to create a climate of confidence and soft euphoria and to cause some physiological mechanisms, such as salivation or the slowing of the cardiac rhythm. Generally speaking, it aims to soothe or even depersonalise the individual in order to direct and increase productive behaviour.

The New Stakes

Some music genres seem to have benefited from the present phenomenon of the globalisation of communicative means, allowing them for the first time the legitimacy to spread beyond their usual borders. In civilisations belonging to the developing world in the global economy, the ear lent by the stranger – that is, by the empowered stranger – contributed paradoxically to invigorating the practice of arts with a millenary past. This interest caused the merchandising, sometimes extreme, of some 'crystal-clear values'. These corresponded to international market criteria and were dictated by the fashions and tastes of a large public. Despite the fact that many performers were of modest quality, it offered them the opportunity to present their art abroad.

According to a simplistic vision, the African plays the drum, and thus he has it in his blood; the Indian from the Andes loves the wind and the sentimental, monotonous chant of the reed flute; the Gypsy knows how to move us with melismas of his overflowing soul; and the Oriental enjoys showing his mystical tendencies in interminable improvisations with hypnotic properties. Independent of their talent (which is not questioned), the success of artists such as the Drummers of Guinea, Los Calchakis, Gheorghe Zamfir or Ravi Shankar can be explained by these clichés alone. Some genres export better than others because they correspond to the expectations of their new audiences. Even though they may possibly provide a biased, partial or even simply false idea of a culture, people or whole civilisation, these musical styles contribute at least to reinforcing the reassuring picture created by some; and they have a decided interest in preserving this image of a region of the world and its inhabitants.

Fortunately, today we need not remain at that point, and the music lover's judgement is much facilitated by greater accessibility of the necessary information. In Europe, as in North America and East Asia – that is, in regions with the capacity to take such action – some institutions have begun to develop a coherent and global pathway for the revalorisation of so-called traditional music. This happens not only through comprehensive research and documentation, but also sometimes by sustained action of the music's holders and potential audiences. Over the years, such initiatives have introduced a large panorama of musical practices which, until recently, remained pretty much inaccessible to non-specialists, and which have substantially modified our way of thinking about, producing and discerning music in general.

By reinforcing the sense of cultural belonging and the legitimate pride of some performers, international appreciation for these musical genres has allowed some of them to survive transformation or even evade the decay and impoverishment of their environment. However, the effects of such a line of thinking are not durable enough to fully take into account the totality of parameters of musical expression. It is not sufficient to preserve art forms by privileging their most prestigious performers; it is necessary also to question what should be done in order to ensure the conditions necessary not only for maintaining, but also for developing or even renewing the music's practice in contemporary society.

In the eyes of its collectors, this valorisation of traditional music can be seen in different ways. Their most urgent concern is evidently the music's transmission, which no longer happens through the normal ways – it may be attended to, for example, by the circulation of audio documents. In this respect, the systematic collections recorded by ethnomusicologists prove to be of vital importance. It is also desirable to create new prospects, in situ and abroad, for those musical categories considered 'at risk'. The creation of centres for the preservation and performance of traditional arts has already seen its success in certain countries. Furthermore, the establishment of international networks of recognition, notably in Europe, plays a role today that is far from negligible in the transmission of traditional genres and the recognition of their inherent values.[3] To distinguish this music from modern world music, these institutions typically apply certain precise criteria in choosing guest artists:

- authenticity: artists are considered representative of their culture;
- quality: they are qualified and, when possible, according to the opinion of competent people, are among the best of the kind;
- exportability: they are 'exportable', meaning that their performances, once transposed out of context, retain as far as possible their full significance and do not appear either to be misused or to incite cultural voyeurism.

Each of these criteria is clearly a topic of debate: who is indeed really able to judge the authenticity, quality and exportability of an artist or a musical ensemble? What is it important to present from a culture, and how should one go about it? Is it necessary, for example, to avoid inviting certain ensembles or musical genres because they would not be spectacular enough? If so, one manages to condemn them to silence under the pretext that they do not 'make the grade'. Is it necessary to reject the use of amplification or of modern and electronic instruments in these genres because these means are not traditional? When applying excessively narrow selection criteria, cultural experts responsible may expose themselves to the criticism of holding overly purist attitudes, or even becoming dictatorial. If a movement of 'early music' has to

---

3   Among the first specialised institutions in Europe to invest in this area are the Maison des Cultures du Monde in Paris, the Royal Tropical Institute in Amsterdam, the Ateliers d'ethnomusicologie in Geneva and the former International Institute of Traditional Music in Berlin.

establish itself in other cultures as it has in Europe, this movement should logically emanate from the performers themselves, not from foreign promoters anxious to see these genres matching an image they themselves have created and want to spread.

All judgements of value are evidently subject to validation in the domain of cultural appreciation; systematic opposition always proves to be fruitless and leads to dead ends. It would be just as absurd to want to hold exclusively to a traditional image of other cultures of the world as it would be to live content merely in the immediacy of their modern production. The great paradox of present times is perhaps the tendency for the standardisation of cultural models which goes together with a marked capacity for the absorption of the most diverse influences and which leads some to drop their own traditions, turning instead toward those of others.

The taste for the practice of certain music taken out of its cultural context is occurring in a spectacular way. One hears too often that music is a universal language, but without specifying what music one is referring to, such that it becomes obvious that the comment is about one's own. This ordinary position seems amply testified to today by the fact that one meets performers all over the world fully qualified in Western classical music, jazz or rock. But the reciprocal, if it is true, is only rarely accepted. As soon as it is about *flamenco* or Gypsy violin, African percussion or Indian *sitār*, someone will retort that 'they have it in their blood', that 'it is necessary to have been born in that place' to play like that. What is going on here? Is there a universal music accessible to all, and yet other music that is 'intransmissible' because it emerges from innate predispositions?

So far, it is obvious that music is not in any sense a genetic given, but that it always follows cultural acquisition. The only innate faculty in this domain is perhaps the vague notion of so-called talent or musical gift, which is an individual and non-collective predisposition, a greater or lesser capacity to seize the outcome of an experience and then exploit its potential according to given conventions. So, as many cases confirm, an Egyptian or a Chinese person can become a European classical music virtuoso; the inverse is necessarily true too, and there are indeed several examples to demonstrate it.

Thus, and if we want it to attach to the reality in which we live, we are required to re-evaluate the notion of culture, and notably that of musical culture. The emergence of new and cosmopolitan music all over the world is not really related to the beautiful logic of 'ethnic' and traditional genres. They are certainly the products of culture, but of a culture undergoing mutation, constantly oscillating between requirements of the local and those of the global. The internationalisation of musical languages corresponds not only to the imposition of the global on the local, but above all to the appropriation of the global by the local; that is to say, the uses and adaptations of the technologies and processes of modern diffusion serve ends determined by the needs of every culture, of every human group.

Chapter 2

Shared Listening
An Ethnomusicological Perspective

Epistemological Questions

Ethnomusicology is today a fully fledged discipline, which was born at a time of a humanist, scientific and artistic concern to study the music of the world, to inventory it and to contribute to our knowledge of the societies from which it emerges. Ethnomusicology – long considered either the poor relative of 'classical' or historical musicology or some sort of sub-annexe of social and cultural anthropology – finally stepped forward in its own right. Indeed, ethnomusicology has developed a set of analytical methods specific to the musical domain, with parameters referring as much to the anthropological perspective as to the musicological approach.[1] Schools of thought have blossomed, and confronted and complemented one another. Researchers' travels have increased extensively and genres once unrecognised or unknown have become accessible, thanks not only to the multiplication of publications and accompanying technology and media, but also to the international tours of some of their most famous interpreters.

However, ethnomusicology as a discipline is not by definition the study of 'other' musical cultures. It does not refer to a particular field of application that would arbitrarily group together all 'non-Western' and folk music; rather, it corresponds to a set of methods that permit us to take into account all parameters of a musical act, whatever they might be. It is thus possible carry out an ethnomusicological study on a symphony orchestra, a techno-music milieu or rave parties, as well as on the Karnatak tradition of India and the world of the Bambara griots[2] of Mali.

The term ethnomusicology, as we understand it, implies a relation between music and society. It is a dual discipline, reflecting a certain tension, or at least bipolarity, between two more-or-less explicit logics, between two distinct frames of reference. Ethnomusicology results from the confrontation and overlapping of two cognitive approaches that we can consider irreducible; its theoretical and practical validation is located in the wrench between the two, as indicated by the juxtaposition of the prefixes 'ethno-' and 'musico-'. Is it a case of contradiction or solidarity? The question has been put forward regularly, and a large number of methodologies is

---

1   About this, John Blacking wrote: 'If some music can be analyzed and understood as tonal expressions of human experience in the context of different kinds of social and cultural organization, I see no reason why all music should not be analyzed in the same way' (1973: 31).

2   Travelling poets, musicians and storytellers.

now offered to the researcher: from the field of anthropology of music started by Alan P. Merriam (1964) and developed notably by John Blacking (1973), to that of comparative musicology where one of the pioneers was Alain Daniélou (1959) or the purely musicological analysis affirmed by Simha Arom (1991); and from the salvage ethnomusicology launched by Gilbert Rouget (1985) to the participant approach recommended by Mantle Hood (1960)[3] and developed by many researchers such as John Baily (1988) or Jean During (1994b).[4]

Whatever it is, the definition of ethnomusicology rests on this double nature. On the one hand, every musical system is a language in itself, the analysis of whose structures, rules and mechanisms is liable, through the specificity of its object, to illuminate our general understanding of music. On the other hand, there has never existed 'pure' music in the sense of 'art for art's sake' – all music, or the set of what we discern as such,[5] is the product and expression of culture. On this subject, Blacking wrote (1973: 4–5): 'We need to know what sounds and what kinds of behavior different societies have chosen to call "musical"; and until we know more about this we cannot begin to answer the question, "How musical is man?"' As 'humanly organized sound' (ibid.: 10), music is a bearer of meanings insofar as it exhibits and necessarily demonstrates a set of values and behaviours that the society that generates it would otherwise lack.

Some expect to see in ethnomusicology the study of musical genres that are by definition timeless and unchangeable in their expression. They forget that if music is the expression of culture, it is also necessarily the expression of society and the individual within it, and that here the individual plays a major part. There is no more 'music without history' than 'society without history': like every human fact, musical expression shows a constant dynamic between what proceeds from a cultural acquisition and what results in new creations, particular evolutions or external contributions. The nature of a tradition – musical in this case – is not to preserve intact a heritage from the past, but to enrich it according to present circumstances and transmit the results to future generations. Just like a spoken language, a music is an idiom and, as such, a living organism in constant mutation. Therefore, a musical tradition constitutes at one and the same time both a normative setting and a chain of transmission. The creative dimension is always present insofar as, consciously or not, the individual imprints the mark of his or her own subjectivity, feeding in the element of personal talent. In the same way, context acts on the individual, with the individual modifying its content, and choosing whether or not to respect its conventions and rules in practice.

---

3   See also Giuriati 1995.

4   See also Le Bomin 1998.

5   It has been proven that numerous languages spoken by people exercising what our conventions define as music do not possess a term that serves to define this concept. This condition is highly meaningful, being a clue that has permitted us, in every case, to make progress in our musical investigations.

Conceptual Frames and Technological Tools

As much as conceptual frames, large-scale universalistic theories have marked the development of human sciences in the twentieth century and deeply influenced ethnomusicological thought and research. Mainly originated by preoccupations of ideological order rather than by lessons from fieldwork, each of these theories corresponds to a particular movement of scholarly inquiry in fashion at a particular moment, and to the ideological and intellectual climate within which it emerged. Thus, the ethnomusicological literature has been influenced, in a parallel or complementary way, by the visions of the world and of humanity offered by evolutionism, diffusionism, functionalism, comparativism, culturalism, structuralism or semiology.[6] Although these theories are probably useful as reference points in the development of our cognitive methodology, they are, however, globally inconvenient. They apply specifically Western models of thought with their historical connotations to the assessment of data proceeding from another culture.

The problem laid out above is definitely this 'unconscious tendency to project ourselves onto others', which Tzvetan Todorov calls 'scientific ethnocentrism' (1993: 8). 'The stranger only sees what he knows,' says a Ghanaian proverb.[7] Accordingly, a large number of ethnomusicologists and anthropologists have taken pains to recognise the extent to which their path is conditioned not only by requirements of the academic institution that employs them, but also by their own intellectual background. This background is a priori neither better nor worse than any other, in particular than that of the individuals – and, therefore, of the cultures – whom they observe. Even though the ethnomusicologists' good faith is not in question, their disciplinary assumptions do not constitute in themselves an absolute guarantee of the relevance of their work and findings, or even of this work's methodological validity.

Regarding the use of technological tools in ethnomusicology, these have permitted us to develop an increasingly refined and differentiated analysis and representation of our object of study. But, in certain cases, research seems to be more 'caused by' than 'served by' the technical possibilities of its tools.[8] Without overlooking the merit of their results, the use of these tools itself risks distorting the nature of field relations between the observer (heavily laden with devices) and the observed (fascinated by technological apparatus, even if often they cannot grasp its purpose or scope). The observed is thus reduced to the role of guinea pig, or even of the object-pretext of experiments whose ownership and achievement mean nothing to them. The ethnomusicologist must be conscious in any case that their presence in the field contributes to modify the perception that people have of their own music.

---

6 For a definition of these terms see Bonte and Izard 1991.

7 Cited by Vincent Dehoux (1996: 131).

8 The works of Charles Seeger and his collaborators produced from Melograph data; and then in France the work of researchers using the Sonograph from the Musée de L'Homme in Paris and of those of the LACITO archive (Langues et Civilisations à Tradition Orale) on the basis of coupled tape recorders and 'field samplers' illustrate this movement. The use of informatics is generalised in analytic and statistical studies relevant to ethnomusicology.

If the West invented ethnomusicology in order to answer some of its queries on musicality, it is, on the other hand, other civilisations that produce most of the music on which researchers lean and that beyond doubt retain the key to understanding these genres. Does the ethnomusicologist have to neglect assumptions and personal intuitions in order to try to restore *only* the truth of the other? And, do those who take up such a stance consider thenceforth that they aim to translate this truth in a language that is not the language of the other being studied, that does not correspond to its logic or ways of expression? The attitude of certain representatives from the Australian Aboriginal milieu is to proclaim their right to consultation, and request that a 'research protocol' is established unanimously between researchers working in the field and their own representatives;[9] this is a sign of the uneasiness felt by some of the 'observed' facing their observers. It remains to be seen if such a protocol would be likely to cause a greater objectivity in the relation of facts, or if it would risk paralysing the relational dynamics of the exchange.

In an article by Monique Desroches and Brigitte DesRosiers (1995: 8) the debate is put in these terms:

> The anthropology descended from the colonial period retains its influence today by continually placing back in question its heuristic categories, perspectives, and its right to interrogate this Other and to speak of him. Would the voice of the researcher from a European tradition carry traces of inequalities between peoples as if it had forged them itself? The ethnomusicologist nearly became silent; at a given time the temptation was strong to assign no value that did not emerge from the informant's speech alone.

The pertinent issue in this affair does not seem to me to be to know who has the right to speak, but rather what are the presumptions and intentions of the person who speaks, what and how it is that he or she expresses, and to whom the speech is addressed.[10] In this respect Todorov (1993: 74) tells us:

> If I succeed in communicating successfully with others, I have to imagine a frame of reference that encompasses their universe *and* my own. Aspiring to establish dialogue with 'others' who are increasingly remote, we must indeed postulate a universal horizon for our search for understanding, even if it is clear that in practice I shall never encounter universal categories – but only categories that are *more* universal than others.

Towards an Applied Ethnomusicology?

Recently, a journalist asked me, with a certain bluntness, what purpose ethnomusicology served, if it was not simply to satisfy the need for self-justification of a social science that appeared to him to lack any handhold on reality. It seemed to

---

9   See Ellis 1994: 13–20.

10   In this respect, the narrative procedure of 'field notebooks' used by ethnomusicologists such as Bernard Lortat-Jacob (1995), Theodore Levin (1996) or Vicent Dehoux (1996) seems to me particularly well adjusted to the communication of field experiences, insofar as it affirms bluntly the human dimension and the essential contribution of the researcher's subjectivity.

him indeed that the current impact enjoyed by some 'world music' has imposed itself in spite of ethnomusicologists – or, in any case, independently of their influence – rather than thanks to them! My attempts to explain the merits of fundamental research, systematic gathering and formal analysis did not succeed in convincing him, any more than did my conviction of the validity of ethnomusicology as a privileged means of approach to every society or human group, so much did it seem to him that most ethnomusicologists were prisoners of their careers and the institutions on which they depend. According to him, the resulting academic mindset incites them only rarely to worry about the consequences of their work outside specialist milieus; they assume with satisfaction the constraints of the academic setting, conscious or not that this allows them to avoid facing questions much more vital than those imposed by the rules of the game they now follow.

The discussion then slipped onto the subject of applied ethnomusicology, and notably on actions undertaken by some among us, either in the field of music producers who interest us, in order to contribute to their development in the modern world, or, in our own context, working towards the goal of sharing the beauties of our discoveries with others. In his opinion, all this is not what ethnomusicology was about, but rather these were matters of social action and cultural programming, two domains for which, let's face it, our academic studies prepare us rather badly. Is it necessary, in order to appear 'really to serve for something', for the ethnomusicologist to stop being an ethnomusicologist and dedicate him- or herself instead to militant action or the production of performances? In medicine or biology, research has no *raison d'être* insofar as clarifying principles, phenomena and processes unless it informs concrete applications; is this something our discipline would be incapable of? Is it by nature not allowed for us to go beyond the strict limits of the trinomial 'work in the field/analysis in laboratory/scholarly communication of results obtained', or has ethnomusicology – as a 'young science' – yet to develop the full potential of its possible applications?

It is obvious that all social or cultural action needs to be supported by a prior knowledge of the domain in which it applies and that, in the case of 'exotic' music it is the ethnomusicologist's role to accumulate this knowledge and formulate it in suitable terms, so as to provide the necessary information based on a fair assessment of observed facts. In the field, the ethnomusicologist must be an unbiased observer and his or her role is not in principle to imagine solutions to existing problems. On the one hand, there is the survival of musical traditions 'at risk', made fragile by an environment that has become indifferent or even hostile to their existence. On the other hand, we have the interrelated development of musical expressions submissive to the incitements of the modern world, especially in the context of emigration. These two questions remain a blazing actuality, insofar as they translate into the field of music some of the most fundamental stakes of contemporary society. But if they are handled effectively by certain ethnomusicologists concerned with the currents of salvage ethnomusicology and the ethnomusicology of urban and migrating populations respectively, it is necessary to say that they have always represented relatively marginal worries in relation to the dominant tendencies of the discipline.

In a contradictory yet interdependent way, these questions inscribe an important aspect of a domain which, far from constituting an unchangeable observational field, is characterised by the mobility of its parameters. History teaches us that the structures and components of every society – and therefore of every musical tradition – are constantly transforming through contact with various influences; cultural identity is in fact a very complex and heterogeneous notion. However, this respect has become especially critical in the contemporary period, insofar as globalisation puts at issue the validity of all traditional cultural settings.

Which role can ethnomusicology play in this context? Which new orientations should this discipline take in order to answer the challenges of modernity? In a multicultural environment such as that of large Western cities, one notes that world music represents at the same time emblems valorising identities and communication links between communities; they constitute one of the rare domains in which the individuals' integration does not imply the assimilation of dominant models. Music affirms a cultural sensitivity that brings out what is best and more communicative: solidarity, a sense of celebration and shared emotion. Besides, the practice of music 'from elsewhere' attracts every day more and more Western adepts. Appreciative of these genres' technical and expressive dimensions, these incomers discern the presence of certain extra-musical components whose nature at first escapes their attention, but towards which their affinities propel them. Therefore, it is right to provide them with the tools that allow these experiences to be directed in a suitable way.

The ethnomusicologist who is willing to get his or her hands dirty has the opportunity to become actively involved in these new urban zones. The ethnomusicologist's work will then consist in considering the effects of the transfer of world music styles to a new context and, as far as possible, acting in these contexts to assure that the place they deserve is granted to them. But, whatever its importance, this particular option should not lead us to overlook the ethnomusicologist's essential role, which is to study musical practices as artistic expressions and social facts, to unlock their inner sense and then to share the fruits of these marvellous discoveries.

Chapter 3

Tradition in Question
A Problem of Boundaries

Paris, 21 September 1994. We are in a recording studio in Montmartre, waiting for the arrival of a group of Malian musicians. All of them are griots, living in the Parisian region, but belonging to highly respected families back in their country; and they are noted for both fidelity to the historico-musical inheritance of their ancestors which provided them with their knowledge of the traditional repertoire and their talent in its interpretation. Their prestige in the diaspora is patent, and following concert tours in France and neighbouring countries they have begun to enjoy a certain reputation among European lovers of African music. The project is therefore to produce a disc, for which one of their French friends suggests the title 'Bambara classical music from Mali' in order to underline the esteem owed to the high culture embodied by these artists.[1]

Musicians now arrive in the studio and begin to get settled, to unpack and tune their instruments; among these we discover a superb, extra-flat, bright-red electric guitar. Surprised, we ask them if the inclusion of this guitar is necessary considering the nature of the disc we expected to produce. 'Ah! Was it not foreseen?' questions the guitarist. 'No problem, I can use that one; it also works very well.' While speaking, he takes a 12-stringed guitar from its slipcover. 'My father played it before me; it's an African traditional guitar.' One of us asks him if he won't also play the small *ngoni* lute, so common among Bambara griots. 'Of course, I even have two of them here,' he answers proudly, 'a normal one and a special one!' The 'normal' one is effectively a plain, four-stringed *ngoni*, but equipped with a microjack in its soundbox; and the 'special' one is an instrument of his own invention with seven strings on which he has developed a technique that allows him to play two 'normal' *ngoni* parts at the same time.

After a long discussion, we agree that the 12-stringed guitar and the two *ngonis* would be used, but not the electric guitar because its inclusion would cover the timbres of the *kora*, *balafon* and Bambara flute. This solution seems to suit everyone, and the recording takes place with the best overall combination.

It is evident from this anecdote that the choice of one instrument or another is not necessarily meaningful for a musician, especially for a 'traditional' musician like a West African griot. Used to answering various demands, he seems inclined to

---

1   Like the performers of European classical music and of several Asian civilisations, Mali's griots can effectively claim this status (in opposition to 'popular' music) insofar as their music is directly descended from the art of court musicians and was connected to the service of nobility in the old Manding Empire.

accept the requests of these new bosses who are European artistic producers. It is not so much his attitude towards music that changes under the nature or context of these new solicitations that push him to a conservative way of expression or, on the contrary, to a decidedly modern or even transcultural practice. It is not always the same for us, specialists, promoters or Western lovers of traditional musical styles. We often have a preconceived picture, forged by the idea of what these genres and their interpreters should be like.

The expression 'traditional music' is part of today's common language. It defines a realm that includes its production spaces, its audiences and its own specific requirements. Before approaching the question of the representation of this music and the concert phenomenon (which has developed significantly in the past 20 years) it may be useful to attempt a global assessment of the concept of traditional music in order to determine, on the one hand, if it is always a homogeneous and meaningful classification and, on the other hand, what borders separate it from other musical categories, should such a case arise.

Numerous people agree that traditional music genres are expressions of identity, distinct from the 'derivative products' which are, for example, the so-called folkloric music or those belonging to the present world music movement. That is, folkloric music is different from its traditional sources because of its 'arranged', 'merchandised', 'official' or even 'nationalistic' aspects, all of which result from the intervention of external agents. Meanwhile, the label world music is essentially applied to intercultural 'fusion' experiences within the domain of popular music, experiences caused by the meeting of musicians of various origins and by the integration of 'exotic' instruments and sonorities into today's Western electronic musical production. If one wanted to summarise current opinions on these three musical categories, one could say that traditional music is perceived as authentic, folk music as eclectic and world music as syncretic.

Music and Tradition: an Ambiguous Relation

The relation between music and tradition has been for a long time one of the most prominent themes of debate in musicology and ethnomusicology. This question is complex, insofar as the term tradition is itself ambivalent. Indeed, it defines a transmission process, a chain joining the past to the present, as well as that 'which is transmitted' (*traditum*); in other words, it refers to a specific inheritance of a collective phenomenon. If one considers this double meaning, one can say that tradition *is* culture.

To refer to a musical tradition means to consider the set of knowledge, practices and musical repertoires of a society as a coherent and identifiable cultural field, to evoke their role and significance within their context, historical development or stages of evolution, noting marked mutations, significant events and major influences. On the other hand, if one reverses the terms and speaks of traditional music the problem changes because the term now states a distinct musical category. The expression 'traditional music' has entered today's language to designate an extremely large domain of fuzzy limits, a section of 'world music' that corresponds approximately to the extra-European genres little or uninfluenced by external (notably Western) pressures, and to European folk and popular music of relatively old origin.

According to the criteria of author-composer societies, traditional music belongs to the 'public domain'; in other words, the music of 'anonymous or undeclared' authors for which no royalties can be collected, even though World Intellectual Property Organization (WIPO) work groups have relied for many years on the notion of intellectual property and on managing the rights generated by the use of this music.[2] Once legislation and recommendations are approved, the problem of application in every concerned state comes to the fore. Indeed, which entity has the right to claim to legally represent a community? What guarantees, in the long term, that such an entity will respect the holders of a given musical tradition? And, more prosaically, where does the money go?

The problem is relatively recent since it is bound to the market's expansion to include intangible properties that hitherto remained without financial value. It is, in fact, more complex than it initially appears to be because two logics face each other: on the one side, there is the contemporary legal world, according to which all works have by definition an author whose rights must be defended – which is, in itself, quite laudable; and, on the other side, there are numerous cultural traditions in which, for several reasons that will be developed further, the question of the works' author simply does not exist. We have therefore two opposing cosmologies, two incompatible and mutually exclusive value systems: the first claims the primacy of individual rights, placing the individual at the centre of the world, whereas the second affirms the pre-eminence of collective conscience.

According to a common view, traditional music genres are survivors of the past that have remained at a preindustrial stage in their development and have been maintained as living entities either by ignorance or nostalgia. These genres are different from other spheres of musical production in their conservative nature; they are hardly more than a musical trace of the society's past in mutation.

For its supporters traditional music has, on the other hand, a spiritual dimension that some proudly affirm they do not find in the rest of musical production, particularly in classical and modern Western music: they are touched by traditional music's timeless character, by the fact that it seems to transcend the limitations of time and culture in order to reach the most intimate regions of the human soul. Such listeners often equally appreciate the aspect of spontaneity and instantaneous art found also in jazz and other improvised music.

A priori I would tend to share this point of view. It appears intellectually satisfactory and morally justifiable insofar as it puts an emphasis on the respect of identity and the defence of individual cultural specificities. But the problem that arises is one of limits of the domain: in other words, what is traditional and what is not? According to which criteria? And who is entitled to judge the matter?

One may wonder whether several music genres of quite contemporary standing have not already acquired the status of traditional music by drawing on sufficiently long-standing connotations; and if others have retained such a status because their

---

2   Regarding this subject, consult WIPO's website, www.wipo.int, and in particular the section on 'traditional knowledge'.

most recent developments still respect the genre's traditional criteria. Here are some examples:

- music of traditional essence, but played on modern instruments, electric or otherwise;
- music that originated in a tradition, but that is orchestrated and harmonised in Western style;
- urban popular music, such as music from South Africa's townships, Arabian pop, or the music of Indian films or Budapest taverns;
- hybrid music, such as all that of the Afro-Hispano-American domain.

In addition, is Western classical music as a whole traditional in a way comparable to that of India and Japan? Or is its fundamentally evolutionary and individualistic character in a sense the mark of a specifically modern mind – perhaps particular to the Western mentality – which is therefore anti-traditional?

Finally, isn't all music traditional, insofar as each– even free jazz or rap – takes as its basis experiences from the past, from which it draws lessons adapted to its own language, to its own reality? Or should we, on the contrary, consider our modern Western society and the present expansion of its models an exception that confirms the general rule of a humanity governed by a sense of tradition?

According to this point of view, tradition represents either a heavy weight whose effect is to crush individual freedom, or, on the contrary, a body of knowledge whose application can contribute to individual liberation and creativity. Applied to music, art in general or all other domains of human life, this concept of tradition is at the centre of debate on cultural diversity. Can it indeed be dissociated from matters such as identity, religion, development, racism, integration or exclusion, to mention only a few? Its a priori application is therefore worthy of review.

The Criteria of Tradition

Ananda Coomaraswamy wrote in an article on the nature of traditional art that 'Tradition is not a mere stylistic fixation, nor merely a matter of general suffrage.' It is opposed as such to 'academic' or 'fashionable' art. 'A traditional art has fixed ends and ascertained means of operation, has been transmitted in pupillary succession from an immemorial past' (1956: 135). If one believes this author, a traditional art would include its own *style*, characterised by a set of criteria related to its aesthetics; it is the product of a *consensus* shared by the society or group in which it exists; it has an *end*, a *raison d'être* in the setting in which it is considered efficacious, which means that it is not only endowed of a function but also of powers (at one level or another); it includes psychological and symbolic planes so that its efficacy appears through the application of a set of *means*, rules and specific techniques; conservation of data is guaranteed by an adequate method of *transmission*; the traditional arts are finally characterised by the *seniority* of their principles, if not necessarily of all their modes of expression.

A book such as Jean During's *Quelque chose se passe*: *Le sens de la tradition dans l'Orient musical* studies this question thoroughly.[3] The author examines 'how tradition determines itself *in opposition* to other musical forms, in setting itself aside from them, in short, in exercising its power, and thereby leaning on power' (1994b: 25). Intending to determine the common components of traditional music, and concerned as much with its object (music) as its topic (people, human mental and behavioural structures, ideologies, ethics and so on), During separates a set of criteria and levels of relevance shared by this music: 1. tradition as transmission process; 2. content and forms; 3. means of production; 4. performance and listening conditions; 5. social and cultural context; 6. senses and values manifested by music (ibid.: 30–2).

Evidently, the musician's point of view must also be considered and even prioritised. An investigation which began with a sample of representative performers of various origins, all of whom consider themselves connected to a tradition, demonstrates that it is possible to consider so-called traditional music as a specific category within the wider realm of musical production. A synthesis of these data evidences the multiple axes of convergence that as a whole confirm During's analysis. The commentaries on their own musical tradition that most of these musicians offered permit us to draw out a number of general features shared by these styles of music.

- They are of ancient origin and faithful to their sources in their principles, if not necessarily in their forms and performance circumstances.
- They are based on an oral transmission of rules, techniques and repertoires.
- They are bound to a cultural context, a setting in which they have a place and, most of the time, a specified function.
- They are bearers of a set of values and virtues that confers upon them sense and efficacy within this context.
- They are finally bound to a network of practices and beliefs, and sometimes to rituals, from which they draw their essence and raison d'être.

In general, music from the traditional realm – and it is the same for all arts – is of remote origin and relies on direct, essentially oral transmission of its forms, techniques and repertoire. This transmission can vary considerably in its methods, but is in itself the guarantor of authenticity, the link in an uninterrupted chain joining masters and disciples through time.[4] Every artist adapts the received inheritance, developing and valorising it according to personal taste and current style. Not being a simple imitator, the artist is the living incarnation of tradition, as well as its depository and guarantor. The artist also has the duty to transmit as much of it as possible, to teach the following generation, including his or her own personal contributions. That is why the proverb says a master without disciples is like a tree without fruit.

---

3   In French '*quelque chose se passe*' means both 'something is happening' and 'something is transmitted'; see further During 1994b.

4   In the Japanese tradition the prestige of a musical genre may rest partly on its age. One part of the honorary title received by an artist who succeeds his master's rank (*shihan, iemoto*) indicates how many generations the inheritance has been transmitted to since its foundation.

Contrary to commonplace assumptions, traditional music is by definition a living form, endowed of an inexhaustible creative potential, and the bearer of a set of values which confers on it identity, originality and symbolic scope. An opposition between consciousness of progress and traditional mentality is thus inaccurate. It mistakes the latter for a tendency towards unchangeability, immobility and the arbitrary maintenance of forms that often become deprived of content and *raison d'être* by the modification of context.

In an article on musical aesthetics in Java, the Dutch ethnomusicologist Wim van Zanten affirmed that music is 'a way to organise human experience and to express social principles. Thus to speak of music means to speak of social order' (1994: 76). An art or a craft – music being both; one can consider it from different perspectives – emerges from a tradition to the degree that it expresses the norms of a society which determine the setting, the significance and the referential system of either an individual work or performance. These norms refer, in turn, to the society's cosmology, and traditional forms – artistic, social or others – are at once their implementation in their own domain and their reflection or echo imprinted in the human consciousness.

Pushing the argument further, one could say that in music as in all art, tradition implies the presence of an authority guaranteeing the persistence of pre-existing norms. But, when the internal authority which assured respect for the norms – particularly if religious – starts to decrease or disappear, it can be replenished by an authority that is external to the ethnic or artistic group in question, of which one sees numerous good efforts by certain professionals who care about the purity of the traditions that interest them. This displacement of authority involves, it is true, the aforesaid criteria of purity: where those in a religious ceremony might be satisfied with the integration of a modern heterogeneous instrument in a traditional musical ensemble, the ethnomusicologist or the artistic promoter may have something to say!

In order to ground itself, a global assessment of the field of traditional music has finally to take into account the question of the limits of this concept.[5] There has probably never existed a 'pure' artistic tradition. This 'myth' is just as unreal as the one of purity of race, whose fundamental falseness has been demonstrated, if it were necessary, by the perversion of its applications. Far from constituting fully preserved survivals of old times, the arts we consider today as traditional – those adorned with the most archaic appearance as well as those that appear to reveal modernity – are thus the products of multiple contacts and events, of convergent influences whose fusion was achieved through long periods of assimilation; and all this in proportion and according to modes determined by the particular needs of each culture at each period in its history.

---

5   This question of traditions' frontiers has already been discussed in a previous publication (Aubert 1991b: xii–xiv).

Musical Traditions and Historical Processes

The boundaries between musical characteristics obviously relevant to a tradition and those that rather seem to slide away to form a kind of no-man's-land, particularly in the contemporary context, are difficult to define because of the increasing permeability of cultural borders and the resulting reinterpenetration of genres. Within a musical repertoire, a distinction between endogenous ingredients and those of external origin is not always easily maintained or even applicable: every culture is indeed susceptible to the absorption of outside contributions, to the extent of their compatibility, but also to integrating these features into a larger and more inclusive sphere or to progressive dissolution in contact with corrosive influences. In this respect, one may ask a double-edged question: up to what stage of modernisation can a form of music still be considered traditional? And, inversely, what degree of seniority is required to suggest that a genre has become traditional? Is the blues, for example, a traditional form because of reminiscences permitting us to connect it to griots and other African minstrels; or because its existence in a relatively homogeneous form is already more than one century old? Besides, is there a category of blues that remained traditional – for example, that of a Bessie Smith or a Big Bill Broonzy – and others that stopped being traditional due to the introduction of electric instruments, marketing or appropriation by white performers? So, are B.B. King and Chuck Berry traditional bluesmen? And Elvis Presley, Eric Clapton or Johnny Hallyday when they devoted themselves to this music? All of them thought they were, in any case!

Another meaningful example of an obviously recent artistic tradition – although there are many others – is that of *flamenco*. It did not appear in its present form until the middle of the nineteenth century, but its song, dance and guitar-playing components are nevertheless those of an authentic traditional art. In the absence of conclusive documents, various theories have appeared on the origins of *flamenco*, so many that its syncretic character is evident. These have claimed to find the influences of Arabs, Berbers, Asturians and Indians by way of Gypsies, Roman or Byzantine liturgy, Jews or even Phoenicians. To this it is necessary to add the incontestable contribution of Latin America, although this is limited to certain forms called *de ida y vuelta* ('going and returning'). It really doesn't matter. What is of interest here is to note that *flamenco* as we know it today practically emerged in Andalusia little more than a century and a half ago, where it was largely forged by Gypsies; and that, in spite of its successive stylistic evolutions, it has been since its appearance an original and coherent language that synthesised in a remarkable way the contributions of its various origins. It acknowledged the set of aesthetic and social criteria – factual and functional – that characterise every real tradition and already included at birth the corpus of forms and categories that constitute it today: work songs like the blacksmiths' *martinete* or the miners' *taranta*, prisoner songs such as the *carcelera*, devotional songs such as the Holy Week's *saetas* and so on.

There is no music without history, even if it is not necessarily characterised by a succession of periods of grandeur and decadence, such as those Eastern and Western civilisations have gone through. The historic development of a culture is thus a normal phenomenon, which only a narrow-minded conception of tradition would refuse to take into account. The blossoming of a musical style, as in the French

Renaissance, was conditioned by the social, religious, intellectual and political situation of that country then. French Renaissance music was rooted in the spiritual and artistic teachings of the Christian Middle Age, marked by a return to ancient Greek values as transmitted by the Arabian medieval philosophers and, at the same time, influenced by a radically new cosmological and anthropological conception. Because of all this, French Renaissance music could not have been anything other than what it was, and its great masters had to compose under this imposed ambiance as well as according to the faculties of their individual genius.

Although at a different level, it is a comparable historical process that operates when Pygmies of Central Africa borrow the harp or the *sanza* from neighbouring Bantu populations to accompany their songs, when Amazonian Indians imitate flutes heard and seen amongst other peoples of the forest or even when Indian classical musicians adapt the European violin, mandolin or saxophone to their music. Such innovations do not constitute a rupture because these instruments integrate without friction into a coherent vision of the world and its musical expression; their timbres and playing techniques do not imply, a priori, either distress or dependence on a foreign musical system, and their adaptation only widens the expressive and aesthetic range of the artistic tradition without distorting its principles.

Some people hold in esteem the notion that tradition is opposed to all kinds of development or evolution. For them a traditional expression is thus of conservative definition: frozen, incapable of evolving, or even retrograde and reactionary. This opinion is widely contradicted by reality, and when it is applied to societies other than the West it offers a form of cultural ethnocentrism that is itself of a reactionary nature and that the historian Tzvetan Todorov (1993: 63) denounces in these terms:

> We have the impression that a culture is *developing*, and we think we are making an objective judgement about it; in reality, all we see is that it is going in the same direction as we are. Or else, on the contrary, we think that another culture is *stagnating*: this is another optical illusion, for we are in fact only designating the difference of direction between its movement and ours.

Traditional music is not in any case the picture of any original purity, or that of an intact musical past; alive, and therefore subject to change like any organism, it always expresses the present, showing the confluences and stages that have marked its course of production.

The greatest lesson we can take from traditional music genres (as we appreciate them today in their immense diversity) is maybe that they remind us, through the vision of the world and humanity each offers, that all music as 'humanly organized sound' – to return to John Blacking's formula (1973: 10) – expresses synthetically the values of a society or human group. I would even say that traditional music necessarily expresses them, otherwise a society would not be what it is, and music would not be music. The best definition of tradition in music is perhaps the one once given by an Andalusian Gypsy *flamenco* guitarist: 'Tradition,' he told me, 'is a mother who sings a lullaby to her baby; it's all there!'

Chapter 4

The Paradox of the Concert
or The Evocation of Tradition

The Western attraction for traditional music of the world has developed steadily for some time now. Theatres that include these music genres in their programmes fill their auditoria regularly; every year, new networks and festivals dedicated to this vast domain emerge almost everywhere. The popularity acquired by some musical genres offers their most gifted interpreters the opportunity to travel these circuits and enjoy substantial fame. By the same means, the public's field of appreciation for neighbouring genres and expressions that until recently remained pretty much unknown has widened progressively.

As a whole, this cultural movement is characterised by the requirement of authenticity.[1] These audiences are not, a priori, attracted to traditional music genres by the ostentatious potential of their artistic form, or by the use the music might allow from a perspective of intercultural fusion; above all they are attracted by the music itself, its intrinsic value and its stance as a meaningful cultural fact. Such listeners expect traditional music to be represented in an unchangeable way or, at least, in a way analogous to its original reality as regards its performance manner, structures and associated spatiotemporal requirements. When unavoidable, the production will probably be limited to the minimum necessary for the understanding of the repertoire and the valorisation of its different semantic levels; it may also be limited to the suggestion of the music's original milieu, as far as practicable through available artifices and materials.

From the moment it is exported, there is the problem of how to make sense of the referential structures of a music normally anchored to another context and reality. According to a certain point of view, its transfer implies a shift that can be considered in itself a kind of deception, or in any case a distortion in relation to the music's everyday playing circumstances. It is also true that this risk is not present in every situation with the same baldness. In this respect, it is convenient to distinguish different musical, choreographic and theatrical categories within which displacement from the original context and representation pose distinct types of problems.

---

1   For a definition of 'authenticity' within this field of inquiry, see the pertinent analysis provided by Jean During (1994b: 189–209).

Categories of the Authentic

1. Art Genres

The first and least problematic of these categories is the one constituted by the art genres such as those of most Eastern civilisations. Often of religious origin, these music genres have tended to preserve certain features well, in particular their theory, symbolism, participants' behaviour and, obviously, melodic-rhythmic patterns. However, the majority detached themselves progressively from this ritual function within their countries of origin where, through social change, they became 'artistic' expressions comparable in a sense to the music referred to with this term in the West. The transfer of ritual music into court music for the elite, and then into concert music in principle accessible to everyone, is a process that happens in a similar way in different cultures and is marked by a loosening of ties between the musical act and its social role. It can even be seen as a musical demonstration of the global movement toward secularisation and democratisation characteristic of modern times.

Nothing, then, opposes the exportation of such music, insofar as it is increasingly considered a cultural product rather than an agent 'of the cult'. Today, India's and Japan's greatest soloists can be presented in theatres and concert venues in Paris, London or San Francisco practically in the same way as in Delhi or Tokyo: the relation between artist and auditorium is established according to similar codes, with the same conventions and social ritual, and in an absolutely comparable dynamic of stage–auditorium distance.

It is interesting to observe that a large proportion of listeners native to Eastern cultures are no more aware of these music genres than their new Western aficionados. Their involvement often became passive and conventional – like that of subscribers to classical music seasons in Europe – and motivated more by criteria of adherence to a particular social class than by personal tastes. Many Indian musicians are struck in this respect, not only by the genuine and deep interest as well as the quality and intensity of attention that their music encounters in Europe and in America, but also by the actual knowledge of its forms and structures that many foreign listeners have come to acquire along with the capability to identify melodic modes or follow complex rhythms from the beginning to the end of a recital.

These genres are as a matter of course the first to impose themselves permanently in the West, and are among those that acquire the largest adherence. The pleasure of discovering these new sonic universes is allotted to a public that enjoys extremely refined arts – in this respect the music is qualitatively close to Western chamber music. Besides, these genres often include a dimension of spontaneity and improvisation generally absent in chamber music because of the fixed writing of the Western classical repertoire – in this respect, traditional genres are rather closer to jazz. The great master musicians of the East are regularly solicited today by European concert promoters and are appreciated by a mature, enthusiastic and fervent public.

2. Ritual Genres

The category of music and dances of religious character, and in general of all those genres with a sacred connotation or ritual dimension, also attracts a large audience. The incentives offered by this category are at once spiritual, artistic and cultural in kind. The stage presentation of a Byzantine vocal ensemble, a Hindu mythological drama or a Zulu choir has its admirers, even when it broaches a certain ambiguity. Its very manner of presentation raises some criticisms, detractors seeing in it a kind of simulation, profanation and the insidious pull of cultural voyeurism. Furthermore the adoption of codes and conventions particular to the world of stage performance – distance between actors and the public, artificial lighting, sound production, ticket office, interval and so on – may constitute a psychological barrier that some spectators overcome with difficulty because of the production's double nature as neither wholly a ritual nor completely a performance.

The notion of representation is the one in question here, and it deserves to be reconsidered. It is a delicate matter and therefore should not be avoided; one can nevertheless also answer that no one has ever been forced to put on such displays, or, a fortiori, to attend them. Besides, it appears that the reasons motivating the occasional actors of these 'ritual shows' are variable, among which the desire to link a proselytising type of action to concerns of political or economic order might sometimes be an altogether honourable one. Significant in this respect is the case of Tibetan monks, anxious to offer Westerners – who from their point of view live in a world deprived of spirituality – the benediction of the *Dharma* while endeavouring to draw together the necessary funds to reconstruct their monastery destroyed in a fire, and while proclaiming their people's right to regain self-determination and the independence of their country.

'The Tazieh is a religious drama therefore the public is asked not to applaud', one could read in a stand at the entrance of the Park of La Villette in Paris. In September 2000, for the first time in Europe, the Autumn Festival had decided to present a demonstration of Shiite devotion from Iran. Véronique Mortaigne wrote in *Le Monde* on 26 September that:

> In Iran the crowd cries, shouts, hits, dies, boos the villains. Here, in Paris, there is no interactivity. No sobs, tears or outbursts. It's a dry *Tizzies*. Reduced to Western rules (between one hour and half and two hours of performance), … in the absence of subtitles, pre-planned, and facing a theatre group that is not constituted of professional actors, the deprivation of tools helping the public's immediate understanding is a considerable handicap and the proof of a certain negligence.

Another example comes from a group of Turkish dervishes. Some years ago, the master wished to attract new disciples by organising a few demonstrations in the West. At the end of each ceremony he invited the public to come up on stage and start learning certain collective dances. Slowly, what was supposed to be the testimony of one of the noblest Islamic practices degenerated into a kind of tedious and hardly controllable display, overflowing beyond the dervishes' intentions and ending up rejected by most of the public. Nothing is more boring for a seasoned spectator or an admirer of Oriental mysticism than to see about twenty people going up on stage and wriggling without grace under the pretext of exploring an unusual spiritual experience. Sensing the dubious turn of events, the master in question decided to give up this type of proselytisation and dedicated his efforts instead to the development of his disciples.[2]

This story should not be taken for more than what it is: a particular case of deviance. Nevertheless, it is suggestive of the equivocal character of an initiative that can stimulate unhealthy curiosity and behaviour rather than growth and self-realisation. In fact, a sincere internal quest was actually behind the public's interest in participating in these demonstrations, which confirmed their previous intuitions and provoked among those who attended a kind of spark, a turning point, whose full consequences would, in any case, require complex analysis. But it is also true to say that we are here in the presence of an extreme example.

More recently, in the realm of Oriental Sufism, the case of the Pakistani *qawwālī* singer Nusrat Fateh Ali Khan reveals another type of phenomenon: the access of a performer to an artist's 'star system' (without questioning his exceptional talent and charisma); whereas his first vocation was of a different kind, to say the very least, namely knowing how to sing the praises of Islam's Prophet and saints within Muslim sanctuaries. Universally famous through his innumerable records[3] (regularly boosted by frequent tours in the West), Nusrat was the main person responsible for the transformation of a religious musical tradition of esoteric character into a product of mass consumption. Apparently, these unexpected developments in his career did not influence his motivation and Islamic faith, but rather represented 'just a little experiment', if one believes an interview given in 1993 to the *New York Times* (cited in Sakata 1994: 96). However, in relation to the tradition from which he descended, Nusrat represents an outstanding phenomenon, not only because of the disconcerting ease of his talent, but also because of the stylistic innovations he introduced[4] and the mercantile use he made of his music – let's be clear, with his total consent.[5] Some years after his death, one notes that his contribution to the *qawwālī* tradition has been

---

2   This story concerns the Halvetiya Cerrahi confraternity, whose master at the time was the Sheik Muzaffer Ozak, now deceased. The narration of Sheik Muzaffer and his disciples is retold by Kudsi Erguner with humour in his memoirs (2000: 185–95).

3   His records are to be found in the prestigious Ocara/Radio France collection, on Peter Gabriel's Real World label, on the Victor-Japan label or in the set of Oriental Star Agencies Ltd. These records appear among the top sales of all time in traditional music (Baud 1996).

4   It is interesting to note that Nusrat Fateh Ali Khan (1948–97) was the first to introduce the virtuous practice of the solmisation (*sargam*) in *qawwālī*'s interpretation. This practice was traditionally reserved for profane musical genres such as *khyāl*. Such innovation is disapproved of in certain orthodox Sufi milieus in Pakistan because of its spectacular and free character, judged incompatible with the principles of *samā* (spiritual audition) which are the essence of *qawwālī*.

5   But the worse was still to come, as an article speculated on 26 May 1996 in the daily *Le Matin* under the title 'Mirages of the Orient'. The journalist Vincent Borcard notes in relation to one of Nusrat's last CDs, *Night Song* (Real World), that 'the result is likeable, even though it is reminiscent of Jean-Michel Jarre. In the future, duets with Frank Sinatra, Pavarotti or Dalida are to be feared....'

determining to such an extent that today every young interpreter of this genre tends to imitate his style, probably hoping to be as famous as he was.

3. Folk Genres

Another important musical category frequently presented in Western theatres is that of so-called folk expression. Among these, festive music occupies a central place. Bernard Lortat-Jacob states that festivities 'are characterized by contradictory properties, ... they have at once a conservative and a changeable function' (1994: 7). Festivity often represents the point of fusion between the sacred and profane domains; escaping the cyclic conditions of ordinary time, it operates in certain civilisations as an evocation to a golden age; elsewhere, it appears as a collective celebration destined to strengthen social ties as much as those connecting the community to its spiritual references; still elsewhere – notably in carnival-type festivities – a festival is like a temporary and rewarding inversion of established values. Whether or not it is associated with dance, the music that enlivens a festivity is generally speaking of a Dionysian nature – this in opposition to the previously cited art music genres, which are rather Apollonian in their principles, criteria and performance conditions.[6]

At present, festivity music from numerous regions of the world is extensively appreciated outside its original frontiers; it is true that it appears to be more directly accessible, even if the codes which the music addresses cannot be perceived in their entirety. The music does, however, better suit events that suggest the context of traditional performances than do many conventional concert rooms. Even though ensembles such as the Musicians of the Nile, Romanian or Turkish Gypsy orchestras, marching bands of any origin or the numerous active African and Afro-American percussion groups in Europe are well able to raise enthusiasm in a concert situation – an abnormal setting for these musicians – they are nevertheless even more exciting when overseas at festivals, happy pagan and multicultural celebrations to which they adjust ecstatically.

4. 'Ethnic' Genres

Finally, there is a particularly 'exotic' musical category which is often fragile outside its normal boundaries: that which includes the expressive forms of those peoples put forward as 'primitives'. In spite of its ethnocentric and evolutionist connotations, this term serves too often to classify within autochthonous nations – in the sense defined by the international non-governmental organisations (NGOs) concerned with their problems – those populations with names such as Aborigines, Bushmen, Pygmies or Eskimos (Inuit). However, it is necessary to remember that these denominations, as well as the term 'primitives', are all of colonial origin and the people concerned contest them as a whole because of the segregationist staleness they delineate.

How can we apprehend, out of context, the resonant universe of peoples for whom music and dance – or what we consider as such given that these concepts

---

6   See Chapter 6, 'The Art of Hearing Well', for more on the opposition between Apollonian and Dionysian thought.

are not always appropriate to their producers – do not exist except within the frame of a specific function to which their expression is completely subordinated? Their musical practice follows completely different criteria from that of the West, and its aesthetic dimension – for us the most perceptible – can only be judiciously valued through its own codes of appreciation and, more than that, in and in light of its traditional environment.

In this respect, a meaningful example was provided in 1998 through the invitation of a delegation from the Melpa and Huli peoples (two ethnic groups from the highlands of Papua New Guinea) to a festival of music and dances of the Pacific in Europe. The first performance of these artists was marked by some comical incidents. Adorned in superb ceremonial attire, with feather headgear and brightly coloured facial paintings, the dancers entered backstage hesitantly, not really knowing what to expect. Once on stage, they were stunned to see that there were hundreds of people facing them, sitting comfortably in the darkness, frozen in an opaque silence. Speechless, the dancers did not know how to react and showed themselves ill-prepared for the stage. After a brief consultation they exploded in laughter, pointing at the attentive spectators but not understanding their absence of reaction. The ice was broken, and their communicative friendliness was soon shared by the public, which also seemed to appreciate the comical aspect of this unusual situation. The performance could then begin and take place pretty much as normal, yet also in a somewhat incoherent way because of the absence of reference marks orienting the traditional succession phases. The 'show' was definitely well received by a large part of the public, sensitive to this new genre's 'first contact'; whereas it caused the condemnation, or even the anger, of certain others, convinced of the indecency of such conduct.

Evidently, the inclusion of such performances in festivals or concert seasons gives us a lot to think about. What indeed are we able to appreciate about these cultures if we have access only to some of their components (privileged and extracted arbitrarily from their structures of reference)? And what can such a misrepresentation – itself inevitably a reduction of reality – bring to those who have accepted the role of performers? Do they have a way to value the image they provide of themselves? What is its contribution to them? In short, do they have the wherewithal to measure its impact on their overall perceptions of their own culture and its system of values?

From the organiser's point of view it would be questionable to arbitrarily exclude from the programme certain genres, or even performances from certain cultures, under the pretext that such presentations would have a 'debatable' character or are not sufficiently 'spectacular'. Organisers must, however, beware of a kind of third-world paternalism that consists in accumulating exotic programmes in the same way others collect butterflies, without taking into account the specific problems of each case.

When the performances of such groups take place they provoke endless debate among the public: some leave as soon as possible, feeling distressed, noting, understandably enough, that something essential is missing, that 'this will never be as it is over there' and, finally, that the conduct is in itself perverse; others, meanwhile, attend without reservation, considering that their involvement in such events is a rare privilege that brings them moments of incomparable purity or that serves to question some of their cultural prejudices.

Both these positions are respectable and partially founded in truth, even if they are antagonistic. Without being assertive, they show in any case that a cultural entity confronted with these questions engages as much in ethics as in artistic work. The reception of such groups, the manner of introducing them and the place chosen for this purpose are, in fact, of primordial importance; and it is also fundamental to provide those spectators who wish it with documentation that is as clear as possible on the ownership and aims of the performance the group is putting forward.

From the Homeland to the Stage: a Formatting Task

I would like to approach now a very delicate case, that of the presentation of ritual on stage. I know that many people oppose it as a matter of principle; this seems to me a quite respectable point of view but I would like to take the debate further by examining the process on the basis of a lived experience. Recently, I have been involved in the presentation throughout Europe of a genre called *Tirayattam*, performed by an ensemble from Kerala, India. In March 1999, this troupe was invited to tour five European countries, and the resulting experience deserves attention because it raised numerous questions, including some on the ethical plane.

In short, the *Tirayattam* is a tantric ritual performed once a year in certain sanctuaries of central Malabar; it is considered an offering to the god Shiva, the goddess Kali and the ancestors. During the ceremony dancers are possessed by the spirits of these divinities, which bring their blessings to the village community. It is necessary to add that this tradition belongs to just one low-caste kin group, for the incarnation of gods corresponds to what some anthropologists call the compensatory inversion principle. Traditionally, every man in this group learns dance, music and sung poetry. They are also the owners of teachings regarding *ayurvedic* medicine and the use of medicinal herbs, and furthermore of what they call tantric medicine, which includes the knowledge of mantras loaded with power and the practice of oracular trance.[7]

It is interesting to consider the process that was involved in achieving a translation from the sanctuary to the stage. The first question that arises is naturally whether there was any sense in undertaking that process: if it could be considered a respectable cultural representation or if it formed a kind of profanation to be avoided as a matter of principle. Beyond this basic question it is necessary to observe the different formatting aspects implied in this process. Preliminary rehearsals for the overseas tour were carried out over a period of one year and were undertaken in situ with the aid of a local collaborator who was both proficient in the ritual and familiar with the Western context. In fact, this process of formatting consisted in a series of subtraction operations that were systematically submitted for the approval of the master of the *Tirayattam*, the ultimate arbiter on the subject. Here are the main phases:

---

7   Concerning *Tirayattam*, see Aubert 2004.

1. Sampling

Within a ritual event lasting normally 24 hours, sampling consisted in extracting a selection that could be narrowed down to a programme of one and a half or two hours. This selection had to respect the normal development of the ritual, but at the same time emphasise its most spectacular aspects – in particular those related to dance and percussion. It was clear that the aim of sampling was to transform a ritual into a show – a show that preserved the essential elements, but that an external public could appreciate, even without knowing its canon.

2. Filtering

For this same purpose, it was also necessary to embark on a filtering operation which suppressed everything that lacked a *raison d'être* out of context, that would have induced among the public a feeling of voyeurism or that simply could not be adapted to the stage for technical reasons. Thus, there was no real trance on stage, processions were omitted, as were animal sacrifices, and dancing on fire and the use of torches were restricted for obvious safety reasons.

3. Time Reduction

All the main characters had to be introduced so that the performance made sense, but the time given to each individual dance was reduced from about two hours to a quarter of an hour; the artistic task consisted in maintaining all features of each dance in a time period limited to 15 minutes. My friends told me that this work was one of the most interesting aspects of the preparation, because it allowed dancers to become aware of the essential features of each dance. The same treatment was applied to the musical elements, and in particular to the long sung myth descriptions of each deity. Their melodic lines were very repetitive, which seriously compromised the understanding of the words; it was decided to deliver a synthetic version of no longer than three minutes for each deity.

4. Space Reduction

The 'production' had to take into account various different factors: first of all, the theatre stage would be a lot smaller than the dance area of an Indian sanctuary; then, the public would sit facing the stage and not stand all around, as in Kerala. Therefore, the dances had to be partially re-choreographed according to these parameters, and in particular to the exclusively frontal line of sight between the dancers and their public.

5. Issues of Interaction

During the ritual the public is indeed in constant interaction with the officiants. It is not the actors under their costumes and makeup that the public sees but the real presence of Kali and Shiva; the public can speak to them, inveigh, touch, ask for advice and receive blessing. The ritual is an event known to all, where the smallest detail is foreseen and must be achieved in accordance with the traditional model; otherwise it would not be considered efficacious, the gods would refuse to be embodied and the village would have to fear all kinds of calamities in the coming year. The community's expectations are therefore immense, and the dancers and musicians must respect all the established codes; it is not only about their own credibility, but also a matter of the good fortune of the society.

It was obvious that the situation would be completely different on stage: the public would come to discover something new and unexpected; audiences would not know how to react and, for this reason, would avoid intervening for fear of disturbing the performance. It is only at the end that the public would feel able to show appreciation and enthusiasm by applauding endlessly. The artists learned that they needed to come back on stage at the very end and acknowledge the generosity of these strangers: a gesture they would never have made at home and whose sense escaped them, but in which they happily participated.

6. De-ritualisation

One of the essential questions the transference to a stage performance raised is the ritual's relation with the sacred and the way this relation appears when out of context. In Kerala the dance space is a ritually protected area that contains altars dedicated to Kali, Shiva and the villagers' ancestors. Every year, the *Tirayattam* season is preceded by various rituals intended to purify time, space and the community. The officiants themselves retire for 41 days, during which they fast, abstain from sexual relations and meditate daily in order to visualise the deity they will have the responsibility of embodying. It was obvious that these practices were inconceivable while on tour. But it was also clear to those involved that a performance in Europe was not a sacred ritual, simply a cultural evocation. There was no confusion on this matter: all were conscious of the transference the rite was undergoing and were proud to participate.[8] Nothing suggested that their spiritual conscience was affected by this experience, or that it modified their perception of the ritual itself. That is in any case what we can conclude from a set of interviews carried out in Kerala after the tour.

Besides, according to a local belief, if the *Tirayattam* ritual has happened once in a given place, it must be repeated every year in order to update its beneficial effect. Failure to do so risks an invasion of the place by bad spirits. No member of the troupe had the intention of coming back to Europe once a year; on the contrary, they told me that they planned the event not to generate this kind of dependency.

Us and Them: a Game of Mirrors

In general, if a traditional music, dance or theatre performance strikes a Western viewer as an opportunity to meet a culture portrayed in an apparently pure and

---

8   In this respect, it is interesting to note that the altar reconstituted on stage included, instead of a divine image, a simple brass mirror which is the symbolic representation of Îsvara, the 'divinity in itself', supreme Hindu god.

authentic manner, its appeal arises from that viewer's desire to return to origins, enrolling thereby in a more global process of questioning his or her personal value system. The listener rarely surrenders to a performance of this kind as a passive consumer, but rather attends with a desire to become involved in and identify with what is proposed. This desire may be derived from an aesthetic and cultural trajectory, but is occasionally more spiritual in essence. The listener recognises in music 'from elsewhere' lines which guide his or her affinities towards the echoes of an intimate ambition; this music demonstrates an ideal which is normally inaccessible. We look for the confirmation of our own intuitions.

As for the musicians who are selected to play in such performances, they recognise that these opportunities constitute a useful, and sometimes essential, way of promoting and valorising their art. In many cases, the patronage scheme they benefited from in traditional contexts has disappeared or changed to such an extent that they cannot maintain their practices as in the past. The foreign interest appears therefore not only as a welcome stimulation, but also as a substantial source of income. Some genres, mentioned already, owe their survival to their appearance in new venues. The situation is evidently paradoxical, but it captures well the rest of the world's state of economic dependence on countries that have the means to support the luxury of a subsidised culture. Can this interaction alone provide the necessary conditions for a rebirth of musical traditions which are currently fragile due to the haste and brutality of ongoing change, or is it at most a kind of lifebelt, as much providential as temporary? As the ethnomusicologist Peter Crossley-Holland pointed out back in 1964:

> It is easy enough, ladies and gentlemen, to speak of the *renewal* of traditional music, but, without two essential requirements, all this is an empty dream. These requirements are: first, the *renewal of traditional society* itself and second, the *manifestation of genius*. Let us frankly admit that neither of these is at our disposal (1964: 18).

However the situation is today appreciably different insofar as the widening of interest in this domain has become a bearer of new stakes, including those on the psychological, political, social and economic planes. The interaction between traditional music genres of the world and their new audiences develops like a game of mirrors in which each looks to the other for the reflection of his or her own ideal: on one hand, a need for prestige and wherewithal; on the other, a quest for authenticity and openness. This relationship testifies to a redefinition of roles, in which it is not ourselves but the other whom we value as exemplary.

But it would be wrong to believe that a traditional musician is only the spokesperson of a culture's values. The individual talent of great performers past and present plays an important part in our establishing criteria of musical excellence; when we believe we are listening to a performance of an unchangeable and timeless ethnic tradition, what we appreciate is in fact the personal conduct – unique as such – of an inspired or innovative artist within which we may not even be able to distinguish originality (even including the misinterpretation of essential criteria). Whether or not the playing respects the rules of the tradition is one thing, but the presence of talent remains in all circumstances the primary condition for the efficacy of a musical performance. Whatever the culture, the idiom of expression or the place it occurs, the musician remains an artist in the full sense of the term; their degree of creativity and inspiration decides how far they are able to move and convince those whom they address.

Chapter 5

An Artist's Life
or the Challenge of Representation

The Rules of the Game

The stage performance is a representation on three different levels: first, as a playing occasion (music as art); then as a process that evokes a reality (music 'in situation'); and finally as an indication of a totality that includes music and what it manifests (its society of origin and its values). The performance event involves musicians in a new setting, often unexpected and prevailingly profit-orientated, which necessarily influences the musicians' experience. A concert presents a unique opportunity to travel abroad and, possibly, a valorisation within the musicians' own community or even in the eyes of the authorities in their country.[1] While privileging the aesthetic dimension – aural and visual – of the musical fact, and while eluding what constitutes its common environment, this phenomenon imposes new requirements on musicians, of which the first is the fact that they are considered 'artists' and not, as is often the case in their own social context, actors among others in an event where each participates in his or her own way, according to assigned or chosen roles.

The structure of most of our theatres, concert halls and festival venues imposes a stereotyped line of sight that creates an irreducible distance between the artist or artists and the public. The former is illuminated by the ramp's spotlights and the latter is enclosed in darkness and supposed to remain passive, silent and frozen in an almost religiously receptive attitude, except at moments where appreciation must be shown in a long burst of applause (according to the collective degree of enthusiasm).

This status as artist implies that the musicians accept concert norms with regard to style, length and formal quality of performances; otherwise, their message will not be received in its full dimension. A concert is thus supposed to last from one and a half to two hours, and in certain places an interval is imposed halfway through. The performance must adjust to these imperious requirements; if it is shorter, the public will have the impression of not getting good value for money; if it is longer, the room

---

1   Many examples show that a tour abroad can have some positive effects on the future of a group or artistic genre, or even of a community or whole ethnic minority. It represents a kind of promotion in which the country's cultural authorities often become sensitised to the political stakes involved. In other cases it is only thanks to the stimulation provoked by the interest of international cultural organisations that an artistic tradition can escape disappearance; on this subject, see Khaznadar and de Lannoy (1995).

will progressively empty for various reasons: listeners begin to get tired, they cannot miss the last subway, they must work the following day....

The issue of length affects each piece of the programme, which, in order to become appropriate, has to take into account criteria related to the public and their 'tolerance limit'. If a *rāga* interpretation by a great master from Northern India develops in less than 45 minutes, he will be accused of adapting his music to Western tastes; on the other hand, if it surpasses an hour and a half, a good part of the audience will be incapable of sustaining their concentration.

From the moment of acceptance of the concert's norms, it is implicit the musician is representative and therefore cannot require that things happen on stage in the same way they do at home. For example, how can an Asian bard or an African storyteller expect to maintain the attention of a public that does not understand the language he or she is using during a complete epic song lasting three long hours? Still, if the artist has a psychological grasp of these conditions and a previous familiarity with the reality of the stage setting, then a series of concessions can be made, and adjustment is generally harmonious.

Vocal and instrumental techniques, in principle, have to be compliant to our criteria of authenticity, whenever possible showing no signs of Westernisation; just like audiences for European 'early' music, listeners to traditional music especially appreciate the purity of musical timbres and sounds. A voice including excessive vibrato will be considered acculturated and aesthetically incongruous; an orchestra should not surrender to the use of 'modernised' harmonisation or include foreign instruments, especially electric instruments. In general, a traditional music concert must be culturally correct, otherwise it will be exposed to the fiercest criticism.

Conscious of the public's tastes, promoters endeavour to present programmes that satisfy these criteria, sometimes with remarkable aesthetic comprehension and at other times with a kind of purism close to the absurd. In an article for *Trad Magazine*, Henri Lecomte had the opportunity to set about a prestigious artistic organiser who negotiated the arrival in France of the great Tajik singer Adineh Hashemov and his ensemble. The organiser had 'forbidden the use of the accordion' under the pretext that this instrument was not from Tajikistan and that it did not allow the use of subtle melodic ornamentations and microtonal intervals expected from this music (Lecomte 1992: 28).

This anecdote is suggestive of a certain mindset prevailing in a milieu that tends to apply the criteria of cultural fundamentalism to the selection of artists and programmes, in particular those involving non-Western cultures. An Eastern instrumentalist who offers an excess of arpeggios or parallel thirds in improvisations will be rejected as a musician of doubtful taste.[2] It is possible that such an instrumentalist had never played like that in their country of origin; maybe the intention was simply to please the listeners – a supreme sign of corruption for the doctrinaire fraction of the public – and to come closer to them while showing, certainly in a naive and inappropriate way, a knowledge of Western music.[3] On this subject, I remember the sighs of

---

2   'Too many notes', as Salieri reproached Mozart!

3   The inverse is also frequent, and musicians surrender to all kinds of innovations in their own contexts either for personal taste or economic reasons; they place themselves as

dismay coming from part of the public watching a concert by the Indian *sarod* master Ali Akbar Khan when he thought it was good idea to include excerpts from 'Greensleeves' or 'Au clair de la lune' in his improvisations, which were otherwise of dazzling beauty. What was for him a temporary humorous characteristic, a malicious wink, was perceived by a section of the audience as an intolerably iconoclastic act; and comments in the foyer after the concert were essentially about the prejudicial influences on this artist's genius of his Californian residence, hinting perhaps at the presumed abuses of alcohol and women.

Aural Image and Visual Image

Another well-known feature of the concert of traditional music triggers numerous discussions among the public: the problem of amplification. For certain listeners it represents a complete and utter headache because, according to them, it is an obvious and unworthy manipulation and acculturation of the concerned music. What these people mostly ignore is that the musicians themselves require the use of microphones, either because this represents to them a kind of technological consecration or because its use is widespread at home.

Recent developments of music such as that of the Manding civilisation of Western Africa would have not been possible without an electronic contribution, which permits the mixing within a group of instruments of otherwise incompatibly different volumes. Such a 'classic contemporary' griot ensemble of Western Africa, already mentioned several times above, today includes (almost invariably) the following instruments: the harp-lute *kora*, the *ngoni* lute and/or European acoustic guitar with metal strings, the *flé* transverse flute and the *balafon* – all of which have relatively soft sounds but are associated today with various extremely powerful drums, in particular the *djembe*. Would it be necessary to forbid this music under the pretext that its development implies the use of an imported technology?

As for the art music of India, a chamber music par excellence, I only met one interpreter in 25 years who preferred to play without amplification; he, again, was a relatively atypical musician, a *vina* player, a long-time emigrant in France whose conceptions had been strongly influenced by friends involved in the European early music movement. Otherwise, whatever the dimension and acoustics of a room, they all required microphones. The Dagar brothers, great specialists of *dhrupad* singing, even affirmed that the use of amplification had allowed them to considerably refine their vocal ornamentation, because 'everything can be heard' and it was not necessary to continually force their voices during the rhythmical parts of their recitals, when they used to be drowned out by the *pakhāvaj* drum's accompaniment. There it is – another consideration for our nostalgic censors to think about!

It is also desirable that on stage the musicians' outfits correspond to the expected image of their culture – a necessarily idealised image – otherwise they risk being seen as non-authentic performers. It happens frequently that organisers impose

---

champions of the tradition from the moment of their appearance in the West, in order to satisfy the public they encounter there.

traditional garments on musicians on tour – or even, if these have become obsolete, 'period clothing' redesigned for this purpose. It does not matter if they wear a bow tie or jeans at home: the stage is a place of representation, and therefore of idealisation. It is a matter of tactfully treating the visual codes in the same way as the aural conventions. The late Iraqi lutenist Munir Bashir started his international career wearing a suit and tie – probably trying to be recognised as a 'classical' and respectable artist – but appeared at the end of his career in the West dressed in a splendid *gandoura* corresponding to the sonic aesthetics of his music: an eloquent example of transition from modernity to post-modernity!

As for the Chopi of Mozambique, the authenticity of performance of the remarkable *timbila* xylophone ensemble led by the master Venancio Mbande has lately been questioned by certain people because the musicians and dancers appeared on stage dressed in cotton T-shirts and nylon tracksuits of colours judged as aggressive – those of the national flag! Obviously, what these 'authenticity police' did not know is that for several generations the members of this group – all amateurs, in the best sense of the word – have been recruited from among the Mozambican emigrant minority in South Africa; to appear dressed in loincloths would be for them just as incongruous as a contemporary Mozart interpreter coming on stage in a lace jabot and a powdered wig.

The reconstruction of a ceremony on stage – a wedding with a pretend bride, village festivity with a simulated feast, ritual with a sham trance and so forth – is, on the other hand, often poorly perceived. (I have seen this regularly.) A fraction of the public has the unpleasant impression of being placed in a voyeuristic situation, feeling excluded from the process taking place before their eyes, lacking the means to participate in it; the reaction is often that such a representation is not authentic, being instead folklore arranged from a performance of traditional character – actually, this is often quite an accurate description, whatever the intentions of the performance's artists and 'arranger'.

On this subject, an example is that of a troupe uniting a dozen of the best Lakota Sioux dancers and singers founded by a charismatic chief, with the laudable intention of showing Europeans their customs. Carefully prepared with the help of foreign specialists, the programme aimed to present the maximum number of dances practised at the time of the traditional *powwow*. However, despite the immaculate aesthetics of the songs, dances and costumes, no current flowed between these advocates of Amerindian cultural values and their public, although the audience was entirely on the troupe's side. The reason was simple: each dance was reduced to a brief performance lasting two or three minutes, which left insufficient time for the performers to develop their characters or for spectators to enter the particular atmosphere evoked by each dance. In addition, the programme was incessantly interrupted by a presenter's trivial commentaries, intended less to inform the audience, it seems, than to relax the atmosphere. The artists' intrinsic quality, the authenticity of their repertoire and the purity of their intentions were thus not sufficient to guarantee the success of such an enterprise; minimal knowledge of stage norms and psychology of the European public – often unaware of the American 'show's' virtues – would also have been necessary to avoid this kind of awkwardness. Continually rushed, the dancers lacked the opportunity to invest in their dances; they could do nothing but show them, and everybody could feel that!

Nevertheless, the theatrical representation of a ritual does not in itself exclude the possibility of a real investment by its actors or the efficacy of the ceremony in question. Some Turkish dervishes told me they have felt on stage states of ecstasy absolutely comparable to those they usually experience in their *tekké* in Istanbul, and associated with the collective feeling of devotion generated among the audience. In the same way, a priestess of the Afro-Brazilian *candomblé* – who was invited, together with a group of adepts, to present a stylised evocation of an Afro-Brazilian ritual in Europe – told me she had pretended to trance during all the tour's performances, but that in Geneva, where we welcomed the group, she had really been possessed and *orixás* had appeared to her for the first time since she had left Brazil. She became visibly perplexed about this experience and even seemed to question some of her ideas on trance conditions.

The Wise Handling of Constraints

In general, musicians and dancers adjust without problem to the norms of the stage, proving in this respect to be endowed with remarkable ingenuity; the rare errors in this domain seem to arise more from the oversights of promoters or accompanists than from the performers' misjudgements. Most of them are perfectly conscious of what is at stake and the concessions they (sometimes) need to make if they want their art to be appreciated for its own value; they willingly agree to many of these, often with a certain humour, which does not mean they are prepared to accept any compromise that goes against their principles.

Necessarily, these new opportunities for traditional music genres of the world have an influence on their modes of expression. Performance conditions are different from those found in the usual context, particularly in the nature of relations between what Gilbert Rouget calls 'musiquants' (producers of music) and 'musiqués' (those who receive it). In attempting to analyse the full range of changes caused by this transfer one encounters certain common tendencies, first among which is a propensity to take up a certain purism, as those involved search for a 'correct' visual and aural image that best conforms to the genre's rules; the situation is similar to that applied in contemporary interpretations of European early music – with which, as we have already noted,[4] more than one traditional music shares various features.

The picture Andean musicians give of their culture abroad has, for example, altered greatly during the past 40 years. In an initial phase, one watched a surge of orchestras performing a 'renovated' hybrid folklore, virtuosic and cleverly arranged, whose models were groups such as Los Incas or Los Calchakis; on the other hand, and since the beginning of the 1980s, there has been a powerful return to ensembles based on those of, the Quechuas and Aymaras communities of the high plateau,

---

4   For some time the current of research and interpretation of early European forms has been broadened to look deeply into other cultures, such as the Turkish and Arabian, East Asian (China, Korea, Japan and Vietnam) and even those of Greek or Egyptian antiquity and the pre-Hispanic civilisations of South America.

where the absence of stringed instruments and the wearing of plaits and ponchos are the signs of an identity claim.

On the plane of performance, another contingency relates to the concert's level of exigency, which is proportional to the public's degree of familiarity with the genre delivered. *Flamenco* guitarists, for example, must take into account the prowess of Paco de Lucía, Indian *sitār* players that of Ravi Shankar or Vilayat Khan, and exponents of the African *djembefola* that of Adama Dramé or Soungalo Coulibaly, because they know they will be judged against these standards of excellence. A new kind of emulation results from this, pushing most performers to constantly extend the limits of their technical capabilities. The result is that performance virtuosity has increased considerably in the last few years, sometimes reaching extraordinary heights. But many connoisseurs lament the loss of musicality that results when listening to these musical athletes, more motivated by the quantitative aspect – calculable in the number of notes per minute – than by the quality of expression and emotions their performance engenders.

As in any other domain the laws of competition now apply, imposing their rules on those vulnerable to them. The market's internationalisation represents today a new challenge for musicians who cannot, as in the past, rely on the support of social structures that often guaranteed well-being and respectability within the musicians' own culture. Their fragile status is constantly questioned by changing fashions and representative stakes. However, is it not precisely in this ability to shape a real performance from the 'good use' of constraints that the nature of a true artist resides?

Chapter 6

The Art of Hearing Well
A Sketch-Typology of the Listener

Jean-Jacques Nattiez wrote that, 'If we acknowledge that sound is not organized and conceptualized (that is, made to form music) merely by its producer, but by the mind that perceives it, then music is uniquely human' (1990: 58). In this particular case, and having already examined the influence of the new *situation* represented by the concert on the parameters of musical *emission* of music genres which are a priori not destined to be performed in such a situation, it is convenient to confront these parameters with the complementary ones of musical *reception*. Generally speaking, the latter is conditioned by many factors, depending as much on the personalities of the 'receivers' as on those of the 'producers' and the circumstances in which their relationship is established. There is no exact match between what Nattiez calls 'strategies of production (poietic)' and 'strategies of perception (esthesic)' (ibid.: 67); and the interdependence of these factors appears to take the form of a complex network of analogies – individual and collective – between producers (*musiquants*) and receivers (*musiqués*). When confronted with the same event or *aural object* – musical or not – *subjects* may discern it in different ways according to a range of personal determinants. Pierre Schaeffer calls this the 'intentions of perception' (1996: 114). Among these he distinguishes 'two pairs of characteristic listening tendencies: the first is about opposing natural listening to cultural listening, the second compares banal listening with specialised or expert listening' (ibid.: 120). Another distinction, a more relevant one, consists in dividing listeners into two categories concerning their attitude towards music: distant listeners, whose appreciation proceeds from an analytic and, in principle, objective approach to what they hear; and participating listeners, whose listening is of a more synthetic nature, fed essentially by aspirations of a subjective and emotional order. The first type is especially susceptible to the forms and structures of music; the second, to its content and effects.

For every musical performance to an audience, a reciprocal subject–subject relationship becomes established between musicians and listeners, insofar as the nature of reception conditions that of emission. Consciously or not, a musician always plays for those who listen, the interpretation being determined by the conjunction of a set of circumstantial factors: certainly, there is personal disposition, the psychological conditions created by the surrounding circumstances and the public's receptivity and reactions – ostensible or not, but always perceptible – to the music. Except in solo performance, a musician is in intimate interaction with the other musicians too, whose complicity exercises a major influence on individual playing; as for the listener, perception is also changed by other surrounding listeners.

Hence, three interdependent relational arrangements appear: musician to musician, musician to listener (and vice versa) and listener to listener.[1]

In the best scenario, the optimal conditions of emission, reception and situation are united and a kind of state of grace results – a privileged moment that every musician or music-lover remembers as a period of enchantment. Characterised by a particular 'presence', 'inspiration', 'flavour', 'ecstasy', 'ravishment', this state is attested to in numerous cultures. Concepts such as *rasa* in India, *hāl* in Iran, *tārab* in the Arabian world, *dor* in Romania, *duende* in Andalusia, *saudade*[2] in Portugal and Brazil or even the Afro-American *blues* are comparable to this kind of paroxysm, which comes from the power of an art, and that of music in particular, and whose effects appear in comparable ways on both its producers and receivers. In this state, the musician becomes one with his instrument, and the music takes him over, moved as if by a force beyond his own will. Just as listeners do, the producer becomes now a receiver, an object of music's 'enchantment'. Without entering into the details of this process, the modes of which have already been studied in depth within the context of Persian Sufism by Jean During,[3] we can restrict ourselves to mentioning only that it is comparable to an ethos or a mystical type of momentum, caused by the magical character occasionally assigned to music.

Adorno's Typology

In his book *Introduction to the Sociology of Music*, Theodor Adorno starts by defining the discipline in question 'as knowledge of the relation between music and the socially organized individuals who listen to it' (1976: 1); he aims to study 'theoretically with typical modes of conduct in listening to music under the conditions that prevail in present-day society' (ibid.: 3). Considering musical listening as a sociological index, Adorno questions 'the adequacy or inadequacy of the act of listening to that which is heard', and, for this purpose, distinguishes seven mutually exclusive listening types, which he considers 'qualitatively characteristic profiles' (ibid.: 4–17):

1. The *expert* 'would have to be defined by entirely adequate hearing. He would be the fully conscious listener who tends to miss nothing and at the same time, at each moment, accounts to himself for what he has heard'; this is how 'the fully adequate mode of conduct might be called "structural hearing".'

---

1   For an approach in the field of anthropology of the theatre and performance studies see Pearson (1996).

2   It is interesting to note that *saudade* comes from the Arabian *sawda*, which means 'nostalgia', 'melancholy'.

3   Regarding hāl in the Persian context, which is defined as being a '"temporary alteration of the state of consciousness", an "exit from the normal state", but in a valuable sense' (During 1994b: 162), this author says that 'hāl's most important stakes seem to be, on one hand, the fusion and unification established between producer and music, and, on the other hand, its propensity to open the routes of creation' (ibid.: 165).

2. The *good listener* 'makes connections spontaneously, and judges for good reasons, not just by categories of prestige and by arbitrary taste', he 'understands music about the way we understand our own language even though virtually or wholly ignorant of its grammar and syntax. ... This is the type we mean when we speak of "a musical person".'

3. The *culture consumer* is 'a voracious listener ... well-informed ... a collector of records. He respects music as a cultural asset, often as something a man must know for the sake of his own social standing. ... On the whole, his relation to music has a fetishistic touch. The standard he consumes by is the prominence of the consumed.'

4. The *emotional listener*, a type which 'extends from those whom music, of whichever kind, will stimulate to visual notions and associations to men whose musical experiences approach the torpor of vague reveries; ... the emotional listener considers music a means to ends pertaining to the economy of his own drives.'

5. The *resentment listener* 'scorns the official life of music as washed-out and phantasmic', and is 'seemingly nonconformist in his protest against current musical activities, the resentment listener will mostly sympathize with orders and collectives for their own sake, along with all socio-psychological and political consequences.' He 'clings at the same time to the ideology of social eminence, of elitism, of "inner values".'

6. The quantitatively most significant type is the listener to whom *music is entertainment*. He 'is the type the culture industry is made for, whether it adjusts to him, in line with its own ideology, or whether it elicits or indeed creates the type; ... music for him 'is not a meaningful context but a source of stimuli.' The relation with music is comparable to an 'addiction.'

7. Regarding the type of the 'musically *indifferent*, the *unmusical*, and the *anti-musical* – if we may combine those in a type', the author limits himself to the hypothesis in which the reactive character of such behaviours could be due to reasons of a traumatic nature.

The Taste for The Other

In the typology summarised above, Adorno considers in essence listeners of Western classical music, referring occasionally to jazz-lovers – within the 'resentment listener' type – and the 'standard merchandise' of pop music. He ignores, on the other hand, listeners to music from cultures other than ours, for the simple and good reason that in 1962, the date of the first German edition of his work, they represented only a handful of people; and concerts, discs and radio and television broadcasts including this musical domain were extremely rare.

The increase in music on offer since then to include a considerable number of genres formerly practically inaccessible and unknown has been accompanied by the formation of new categories of audiences with new musical tastes. Conscious of the beauties and meanings of such-and-such an 'exotic' music, or even attracted by different forms of hybridisation or fusion, 'ethnomusic-lovers' constitute one of the most meaningful 'alternative currents' of the contemporary period. However, amateur listeners to world music do not represent a unique category; their orientations and incentives are probably as various as those Adorno states, and largely intersect with them anyway. However, they also include their own specific characteristics: for example, those determined by the nature and geocultural orientation of individual tastes, as well as the psychological, social or intellectual causes underlying these tastes.

- If one considers the *expert* type, nothing distinguishes the listener to traditional music from that of European classical music, apart from the object of his or her predilection. This listener is especially characterised by high requirements concerning authenticity of performance and repertoires, which must correspond in the first place to the genre's canon.
- The *good listener* type, already familiar with what he or she hears, includes a wide range of examples, from the 'transcultural' – following a personal trajectory of immersion in a foreign culture, this listener has acquired its codes and therefore reacts more or less as a member of that culture – to the simple, open music-lover, who has developed affinities above all through listening and is receptive to everything that constitutes the music of his or her interest.
- The *culture consumer* is a common type among traditional music-lovers. The collector's spirit is shown by a desire to capture everything, a thirst to augment his or her field of musical experience, often associated with a systematic tendency towards superficial comparative studies. Music is of interest if it confirms the idea she or he has of it so far.
- The *emotional listener* is less interested in a genre's cultural dimension than in its sensory stimulation. It is above all personal fantasies that are projected, even though the listener believes that he reacts as a native. The dreamlike effect that a genre provokes is sometimes deliberately accentuated by the use of psychotropic substances, which are supposed to put the listener 'in phase' with the privileged moment that musical performance represents.
- The *resentment listener* is also a widespread type: the nonconformist who expresses him- or herself more freely, believing to have discovered the 'radical other'. This listener is a *spirit adventurer* who searches in these music genres for an original connection with the world. Listening represents an interior journey, and its attraction is proportional to the desire to question personal cultural habits and to open up new perspectives. The attraction for such-and-such a music frequently doubles as an idealisation of the musical performer's presumed lifestyle, which appears equally as a dismissal of the values of the listener's own culture.
- The person who listens to exotic music as *entertainment* is essentially enthusiastic about the atmosphere created and the occasion where it is presented or the memories that it evokes – those, for example, of a book, film or vacations passed in the country of origin. Music is nothing more than a pretext, and this type of listener expects nothing from it but an aural environment corresponding to his or her feelings or excitement.
- Regarding those who are *indifferent* to music from elsewhere, who do not

feel for it or are against it, they correspond to four distinct categories. The first is the *physiological* type – the person who 'doesn't understand anything' (whatever the music) or who considers these genres uninteresting because of their presumed poverty or monotony. The second is the *relational* type – the absence of references blocks access to these genres, so that the meaning cannot be understand; or what is understood does not correspond to the real message. Regarding this topic Umberto Eco speaks (in one of his texts about rhetoric) of an '"abnormal" interpretation' that leads the receiver to 'receive a message in a psycho-sociological situation that is not foreseen by the producer. The message is founded on codes, subcodes and the receiver's supposed knowledge, which the receiver does not in fact possess; this receiver refers on the contrary to private codes, other kinds of semantic fields or to the sudden impact of aleatory connotation, and is often a victim of deviant circumstances' (1984: 166). The third category is the *psychological* type – these music genres disturb such a listener by their weirdness; he or she rejects them before considering them. As for the fourth of these categories, it is the *ideological* type – the dismissal here is more than anything else a self-defence mechanism to music with possible political connotations; it is of a xenophobic nature, comparable to the famous 'national preference' exacerbated by those of extreme right-wing ideologies.

The Apollonian and the Dionysian

Not having been able to consider transcultural possibilities, the list proposed by Adorno disregards three 'types' of listener that frequently appear amongst those who enjoy music from elsewhere. The first is the *curious for diversity* type, fascinated by cultural difference in itself, who loves to be surprised by hitherto unknown creativity and whose incentives are of both aesthetic and sociopolitical order. The other two are what we could call the *contemplative listener* or, by turning to Nietzschean categories, the *Apollonian*, and the *enthusiastic listener*, or *Dionysian*, respectively. The domain of predilection of the former includes the predominantly modal Oriental genres, whereas the latter will be keener, for example, on African and Afro-American expressions characterised by the intensive use of percussion instruments. Moreover these types listen in various degrees to other musical genres also – the first especially to classical and early music, in particular to chamber music, as well as to plainchant and religious music; the second mostly listen also to jazz, rock and reggae.

For these two types of listener – the contemplative and the enthusiast – the concert or musical event is lived as a ritual. Passing the level of simple sensory or intellectual enjoyment, their listening is of an essentially participatory nature, which, consciously or not, follows a quest for sacredness. For the first type this search appears in a desire for ecstasy and mystical identification with the deepest self; for the second, at the other extreme, it emerges from a willed liberation from the ego's constraints similar in means to that found in trance phenomena. For this reason, I will evoke Gilbert Rouget's distinction between ecstasy and trance, reserving ecstasy 'solely to describe one particular type of state – altered states, let us say, attained in silence, immobility, and solitude', and designating by trance 'solely those [states] that are obtained by means of noise, agitation, and in the presence of others' (1985: 7).[4]

The Apollonian searches for ecstasy as a 'gentle method' working within a continuity logic related to normal states of consciousness; it corresponds to a progress we may call 'melodic' or 'linear'. The Dionysian, on the other hand, is more sensitive to the 'strong method' that represents trance as a process characterised by discontinuity and the 'rhythmic nature', being comprised of ruptures while also organised in a cyclic way. The Colombian anthropologist Jorge López Palacio led me to notice that these two types could also be defined as 'the thirsty' and 'the hungry'; respectively, a thirst for music leads to ecstasy and a hunger for it to trance. He thus proposed a distinction between melody's 'liquid' state – that of a music of melodic prevalence – and rhythm's 'solid' state: that of a music where this is predominant.[5]

It is necessary to mention, though, that these two types only manifest psychological predispositions; however sincere the individuals who correspond to them are, these predispositions will remain latent or will only manifest themselves in a transient way unless they are developed through the acquisition of appropriate cognitive methods, often involving initiation, just as one encounters within numerous spiritual traditions.[6] In a general way, I am conscious of the aleatory character of such a typology, which only distinguishes tendencies and, because of this, exposes itself to the charge of 'fuzzy classification'. It can mostly contribute by focusing on some unconscious foundations of musical taste in Western society; but certain individuals are likely to identify with none of these listener types, which could be extended infinitely. Concerning taste, the prerogatives of subjectivity remain essential, and our preferences answer to determinants that, fortunately, retain a large part of their mystery.

---

4   Ecstasy, writes Rouget, 'is a keenly memorable experience which one can recall and ponder over at leisure and which does not give rise to the dissociation so characteristic of trance.' Trance, on the contrary, 'is characterized by total amnesia. The relationship of the self to the trance state is, in this respect, diametrically opposed to that of the self to ecstasy' (1985: 9). 'Thus trance always manifests itself in one way or another as a transcendence of one's normal self, as a liberation resulting from the intensification of a mental or physical disposition, in short, as an exaltation – sometimes a self-mutilating one – of the self' (ibid.: 14).

5   In an oral presentation.

6   Sufism distinguishes the *hāl* or spiritual 'state' from the *maqām* or 'station'; the first is considered as temporary and accessible to everyone, and the second is considered as steady, reserved in principle for insiders only (see also above, n. 3).

Chapter 7

The Invention of Folklore
or The Nostalgia of Origins

The Idealisation of the Bucolic

Folklore has today a bad press, but no one seems to know exactly why. It has been condemned 'without trial', observes Nicole Belmont in an eloquent article published in the reputable magazine *L'Homme* under the title 'Le Folklore refoulé, ou les séductions de l'archaïsme' (Folklore repressed, or the seductions of archaism). 'No contemporary anthropologist would dare to acknowledge himself or herself as a folklorist', she wrote. 'Slightly ashamed, French ethnology hardly recognises folklore as an historical stage in the study of European societies and cultures. It denies it any scientific value and diminishes itself to the common and pejorative use of the term' (1986: 259–60). But what are the reasons for such antagonism towards a body of thought which is both vast and seemingly worthy of the utmost respect?[1]

Folklore as a discipline appeared at the beginning of the nineteenth century. At that time, a vast collection movement developed, targeting folk arts and traditions throughout Europe. It arose in order to avoid the risk of change or disappearance to which this domain was exposed, in particular because of the effects provoked by national social integration, centralisation and the ideology of progress, as well as industrial revolution and rural exodus. Romanticism was no stranger to this movement, and many writers – such as Mme de Staël, George Sand and Gérard of Nerval in France, or Goethe, Novalis, Fitche or the brothers Grimm in Germany – actively participated in this conservation drive, contributing to the collection of rural traditions and their adoption in order to 'create an original novelistic style and participate in the advent of a new source of literary inspiration.'[2]

In 1852, Louis-Napoleon Bonaparte created and published a decree known as the 'Fortoul decree', named after the Minister of Public Instruction and Religion charged with putting it into action. Written by the historian Jean-Jacques Ampère,

---

1   On this subject, Mark Augé states 'that ethnographic study of France developed in opposition to the folklorist tradition by *localizing* research and envisaging its object as a *totality*.... The reactualization of ethnographic research may be most fully appreciated in terms of its opposition to folklorist ethnography. With their *passé*-ist vision of society, French folklorists had privileged the study of traditional themes whose circulation they examined or whose disappearance they observed without being at all interested in how they were sociologically anchored – that is, without concerning themselves with the localized totalities that would become ethnography's specific object' (1998: 94–5).

2   See Jean-François Dutertre: 'L'herbe sauvage. Perspective cavalière sur le romantisme et les traditions populaires', in Le Quellec 1993: 10–21.

the physicist's son, in the format of a manual of *Instructions on the folk poetries of France*, the protocol called for the systematic collection, notation and classification of the corpora of French folk song and poetry in the oral tradition in order to rescue from oblivion 'the values time carries away every day', the 'examples of beauty for too long unrecognised', which carry the 'trace of events of national history'. Even if the results were qualitatively somewhat unequal, this endeavour put into circulation a considerable amount of data, while being probably the first major action led by salvage ethnomusicology.[3]

The term folk-lore appeared in English in 1846, having been wrought by the mythologist William John Thoms to designate 'the people's knowledge, doctrine and wisdom.' (It was not adopted in French until 1877.) For the Swiss ethnomusicologist Max Peter Baumann, folklore includes 'all the forms of popular expression, folk musics and dances, riddles, whims, etc. … which exist as customs of oral transmission still transmitting themselves from mouth to ear as traditions present in real life.' In relation to musical folklore he adds that this 'does not refer to a theory and does not recognise any musical notation. … In musical folklore one cannot distinguish between those that actively contribute to the musical custom and those that passively enjoy folk expressions.' Baumann opposes to folklore the notion of 'musical folklorism', which consists in:

> representing a folk music custom as if one belonged to the peasant class, 'to do as if' … it is characterised by notated musical pieces which are songs or dances either arranged or imitated. … The custom is studied in performances and musical processions which aim, rightly or not, at redressing and renewing the values of the past.

The promoters of folkloric stage performances have collectively established a gradation in the folklorisation of musics and dances presented at their events. Thus, they distinguish the 'authentic' (or faithfully re-established) from 'elaborate' and 'stylised' groups.[4]

The Ambiguity of Folklore

The ambiguity of the term 'musical folklore' exists because its definition covers several approaches. First of all, in its original meaning this term represents the collection and inventory of oral traditions found essentially in countries where the goal was to protect, preserve and analyse an often threatened heritage – we can recall the exemplary work of Bartók, Kodály and Brăiloiu in Central and Eastern Europe – as well as the heritage itself. Second, it represents the romantic idealisation of music genres with a bucolic character, emblematic of a nation, crystallising a nostalgia for the rural as the sector of society rendered most fragile by modernity, but also functioning as patriotic 'collective memory' on occasions such as feasts and popular performances of the kind of the *Fête des Vignerons* in Switzerland. Finally,

---

3   See Yvon Guilcher: 'La chanson populaire et les pouvoirs publics. Remarques à propos du décret Fortoul', ibid.: 32–41.

4   Here and above, Baumann 1976, as cited (in French) by Renz 1986: 8–23.

the approach is assimilated in 'musical folklorism' consisting in manipulating the folk heritage – as much by political entities as by tourist promoters – for what we might call deflected ends. Here, we can envisage stage performances and orchestrated arrangements by alleged specialists whose task is to make the tradition presentable to an 'external' public, a priori ignorant about this music's holders and ends. Chérif Khaznadar, director of the Maison des Cultures du Monde in Paris, affirms in an interview given to Michel de Lannoy (1995: 48–9): 'This transformation through the external intervention and liaison of a choreographer and arranger eliminates all "scoria" which ... is where the interest of these musics lies, creating instead a kind of sterilised product, a commercial product.'

The stage performance of music genres which, in principle, are not supposed to be presented in such a setting is not, however, a new phenomenon. The first public displays of exotic music and dances in Europe took place at the end of the nineteenth century, in large-scale events such as the Exposition Universelle in Paris, 1889, where we know Debussy discovered with wonder the music of a Javanese *gamelan* ensemble, set up for the occasion on the Esplanade des Invalides. At the time of the Exposition Nationale Suisse, held in Geneva in 1896, different attractions of various colonial origins were again offered to a public apparently fond of exoticism. One of its main curiosities was the 'Negro village' inhabited by a 'Negro African tribe, arriving from Dakar, and lodged in huts. It includes about 200 indigenous from both sexes belonging to various races.' The account of their performance indicates the presence of musicians and dancers, who, 'decorated with amulets, deliver bizarre gestures and ludicrous contortions' (Crettaz and Détraz 1983: 40). Another pavilion at Geneva's exhibition was the Palace of Fairies. It was animated by an ensemble of Japanese musicians and dancers; by 'a troupe from Cairo, consisting of musicians, dancing dervishes, dancers, almahs [Oriental dancers], snake charmers, etc.'; and by a 'Javanese concert-theatre' whose dances were 'performed to the sound of bizarre instruments'. According to a columnist of that time, E. Imer-Schneider, the music was: '... just like the lyrical language of all Orientals, primitive enough. The orchestra, or *gamelang*, has various instruments: a single-stringed violin sounding the melody, gongs, drums and sets of bronze bells or vases of different size.'[5]

Such exhibitions contributed to reinforce the Rousseau-ist myth of the good savage through allowing visitors the chance to admire at home the indigenous customs of faraway countries, in a setting vaguely reconstituted and supposed to represent their natural environment. But in this epoch, such exhibitions did not have a direct relation with the folklorist movement, whose enthusiasts were not interested, on the whole, in anything but the rural expressions of their own country, or even of their own region. These exhibitions provoked, on the other hand, an attraction for the exotic itself, which sparked at the same time collecting and work in the field by many missionaries, soldiers and colonial civil servants. Although the world view of these precursors of 'scientific' ethnology was often blemished with the ideals of colonial mentality, they provided an impressive amount of data and testimonies which offer an indispensable foundation for the elaboration of an historical perspective on societies of oral tradition.

---

5   *Journal officiel illustré de l'Exposition Nationale Suisse,* 1896: 240.

The first half of the twentieth century was distinct in the flourishing of the first national folk troupes, mostly under the impetus of the Communist states, which considered these groups an efficient means of mass education and consolidating sentiments of national cohesion. For the governmental powers concerned, the perversion, codification and mediaisation of musical and choreographic folkloric forms of often ritual origin constituted ideal instruments of propaganda and normalisation. The intervention was to eradicate the substratum of beliefs and practices in which these expressions were anchored, preserving instead the appearance – or rather a counterfeit – depleted of all substance, all metaphysical significance, and wholly detached from its factual context. In 1925, Stalin proclaimed in a speech at Tashkent:

> Of national shape, but of socialist content, such is the culture common to all humanity, towards which socialism progresses. The proletarian culture does not abolish the national culture: it gives it content; and, inversely, the national culture does not abolish the proletarian culture: it gives it shape.

This programme of the edification of the masses equated to a real enterprise of the organised folklorisation of people's traditions across the Soviet empire. However, the fall of Communism essentially demonstrated the total failure of such conduct; it even provoked in numerous regions the sudden awakening of religious, social and artistic traditions hitherto considered, even clandestinely, as places of refugee from the state.

Thus folklorist movements have quickly spread all over the world, to such an extent that every single country has had its official troupes, sometimes used as cultural ambassadors of a national unity, often artificially established.[6] Most of the present-day stars of folk music cut their teeth in such groups. With regard to Eastern European countries, one can include in this category artists such as Gheorge Zamfir and his stable of Romanian virtuosos (later dissolved due to endemic emigration), the Don Cossacks, the Red Army Chorus (which miraculously survived the disappearance of the army of that name) and those who comprised the famous (and very beautiful) Mystery of the Bulgarian Voices, a mystery clarified nowadays.[7]

Regional, national or international folklore festivals emerged nearly everywhere, constituting not only promotion for the performers but mostly a tourist attraction,

---

6   I remember the example of a Rwandan cultural agent who maintained firmly, before the civil war which tore this country apart, that there was no significant difference between the Hutu and Tutsi cultural traditions, and that it did not make any sense to try to find out if such-and-such a musical form came from one or the other.

7   Let us listen on this subject to the commentaries of the music critic Alain Swietlik, interviewed by Eric Montbel: 'First, it is not a mystery. "The Bulgarian Voices" are the kind of classic choir which interprets a classic repertoire of a traditional basis. All compositions are signed by Bulgarian composers. There are a lot of official groups, whereas in France, one is made to believe that there is only one. These Bulgarian groups have a very advanced theoretical formation, working under the direction of composers and conservatoire professors. These women have repeated the same songs since we first heard them, therefore, since 1955' (cited in Le Quellec 1993: 145).

appealing to organisers and local communities alike. With the tendency to encourage the individual virtuosity of performers, musicians and dancers, the most spectacular aspects of the customs were presented, often to the point of distorting, mixing up and parodying the customs themselves. Generated in all performances, these idyllic images of cheerful and heedless people, crafters of an exportable happiness, were revealed in every case in conformity with the greater public's expectations, taken for granted in advance by the principal organisers of these events.

The character of the 'official' artist was thus born under the impulse of folklore academies; trained in all national styles, such a musician often had no contact with the traditions that he or she was supposed to represent. In a country such as Hungary, these musicians – mostly Gypsies, born in the poor suburbs of large cities – were trained by the National Academy of Folklore, which then distributed them according to their expertise, extent of repertoire and degree of virtuosity to classes of artistry A, B, C … . Their workplaces and salaries were determined by the authorities according to this scale; they were regularly delegated abroad and given the responsibility of enlivening national theatres, large hotel lounges or taverns for tourists in the metropolis. It is necessary to note that the downfall of Communism provoked the disappearance of this system and the unemployment of many musicians, who were then forced to move overseas or to shift to other professional activities, the new capitalism of the East for the meantime being incapable of assuming responsibility for them: nostalgia is no longer what it used to be!

Chapter 8

World Music
The Last Temptation of the West

Paradise Lost

World Music

This formulation was launched as a challenge to cultural sclerosis, as the manifesto of all the anti-racisms generated by our sense of historical guilt. It is necessary to note, however, that this term is vague in definition, embracing in principle all 'musics of the world', including the traditional music of non-Western civilisations – even if this word 'musics' is not yet fully established as a plural form in English (although it is found in other languages, such as French). But, in fact, the label world music essentially applies to intercultural experiences within the domain of contemporary popular music; experiences resulting from the meeting of musicians of various origins and the integration of 'exotic' instruments and sonorities with the electronic and computer equipment of contemporary Western musical production.

A foreseeable social phenomenon, McLuhan's 'global village', is rising under our noses and, whatever we think of the script, we are all actors in the social drama it equates. Globalisation of culture is not, as we believed for a long time, an exclusive synonym for the Westernisation of the rest of the planet, because the sonic invasion has been reciprocal, even if we assume responsibility for its initial impulse. Cultural globalisation appears, on the contrary, like a vast and indefinite game of distorting mirrors, in which the other sends back to us the altered image of our transient identity.

We are in the other and the other is in us: how could this reality, alive in our flesh and soul, have remained without musical consequences? Considered for a long time as the *bête noire* of all anthropologies, hybridity is claimed today as the banner – maybe the only one still credible and with the power to call us to action – of a whole generation with aching roots. Musicians understand it well since, having practically exhausted the expressive and commercial potential of the American dream, they turn today with a sincere openness to the delights of a global 'sound world' rich in unexploited resources.

In those laboratories of universal syncretism that are Parisian and British studios, the modern apprentice sorcerers regulate pretty much every conceivable acoustic component: it is even possible to produce the most extraordinary sonorous simulations thanks to the famous electronic prodigy known as the sampler. Thanks to a sophisticated system of digital coding called Musical Instrument Digital Interface (MIDI), capable of storing and transferring every detail of timbre and amplitude, and therefore capable of replicating any desired sound, the simultaneous usage of a keyboard and dial allows us to surpass the limits of our 'well-tempered' music system and replicate the slightest melodic subtlety of modal systems. Thanks to this ultimate gadget the illusion is almost perfect, and the lover of exotic instruments can almost take it for granted. The sounds generated by the sampler are effectively 'natural', but homogenised; they miss the spice given by such essential expressive elements as attack, breath or articulation. But the advantage of this sophisticated device is not in creating acoustic fakes; rather, it is in its faculty to transfer sonic information into new spheres and foster the resources for hitherto unprecedented musical journeys.

World music results from an assemblage of perfectly identifiable factors, not only musical and technological, but also sociological. It is on a par with the largest music movements considered popular in the twentieth century: jazz, tango or rebetiko, for instance. Have not these genres descended from such an enforced meeting of diverse influences? Screaming from a heart that is bursting with fatality, these styles of music translated – and translate still – the conditions of their craftsmen with an implacable poetic realism. They were born out of the misery generated by the modern megalopolis, and it is by singing this misery that they offer a means to dignify and transcend misery. These genres' common strength resides in the following truth, which one finds in the blues as well as in *raï* or *flamenco*: art nourishes itself on necessity.

In this respect, world music is maybe the only original expression that could arise at the end of the twentieth century: it is the summing up of all the 'heres' and 'elsewheres' which have woven our lives. Followers of traditional or 'ethnic' music started identifying with this movement, which promised the flourishing of perspectives based on their tastes. But they quickly lost their illusions; the new product offered for their appreciation in fact corresponded only weakly to their expectations and sensitivities. Music-lovers could find neither the intimacy of a real connection between performer and listener nor the delight stimulated by the gentle touch of subtle intervals; even less the seemingly everlasting and spiritually infused picture they so much desired. The separation was then unavoidable between, on the one hand, defenders of the authentic, of their various kinds, and, on the other, adherents of the great church of musical ecumenism.

Paradise Regained

As a musical bridge between cultures, world music is seen as humanist, generous and revolutionary; it is the crucible of a new age, of a regained paradise in which each has the freedom to express him- or herself, thus, participating in the enrichment of all through the affirmation of his or her difference. However, its humanism is technocratic and its generosity dyed in mercantilism, qualities which inevitably qualify and even tarnish its reach. World music looks for consensus: it tries to satisfy the largest number of people with a product of synthesis. The resulting product, however, offers each of us only a little of our personal needs.

I would like to quote the Irish musician Ross Daly (1992), a specialist in the music of the Near and Middle East and an acknowledged virtuoso of various instruments from that part of the world:

> It would be naive to think that anybody sitting in the comfort of their western European or US home – enjoying a standard of living utterly inconceivable for more than half the world's population – could possibly be able to perceive the rest of the world's music properly, let alone understand it, appreciate it and enjoy it in its respective context, in its language, in its specific forms of expression. I am not criticising the good intentions of thousands of people in the western world who wish to open their minds to other cultures. However, we are a long way from some people's idea of *world music*. The western attitude, marked for centuries by unparalleled political, military and cultural barbarism and arrogance towards other cultures, cannot pretend that equal values and interests exist with regard to the planet's countless individual regional cultures simply because one aspect has suddenly been opened up. I have met *world music* freaks kitted out with all the latest hi-fi gadgetry, surrounded by hundreds of CDs, records, cassettes and DAT recordings, who listen to West African Griots one minute, Japanese Koto music the next and then Bengali music – and when you talk to them about the music, you realise that they don't understand the first thing about the music, that they haven't got a clue about the cultural and human background. What is more, lots of sharp producers are churning out a kind of homogenous world music by throwing together fragments of different musical cultures and blending them with all the available technology of today's studios.

> If we are going to be able to appreciate fully the wide variety of music which exists in the world, we should forget all these recordings and drastically increase the amount of live music we listen to. We should see this as an inner and outer journey, in which any attempt to approach the various musical traditions of the world also has to involve an appreciation of the musicians themselves. It also means being constantly aware that we are all a part of this planet and learning to understand and accept each other in many different forms of expression. We are still a long way from achieving that, and it is still far too early – if at all – to talk about *world music*.

For its fans, world music constitutes nevertheless the outcome of an evolutionary process aimed at valorising traditional music, particularly the extra-European, within the contemporary context. An urban expression par excellence, world music testifies to the creative dynamism and adaptive capacity of its performers. But the ethics of integration have a price: they imply a new North–South relation in which the North erects itself as a model and ideal market for the South. For an African or Asian musician the trajectory required to reach success passes through the gauntlet of recognition in Europe and North America. Rich with this consecration, the musician becomes the bearer of an indisputable prestige, and an individual of unprecedented influence; possible mistakes and personal concessions to international public taste may be looked on by the musician's peers as progress and as qualities they will adopt in turn.

World music is hybridisation elevated to dogma: to be admitted into the circle, musicians must promptly accept the rules of this game of succumbing openly to the intercultural dictate. They have to give up anything too specific that exists in their own musical tradition, in the meantime systematically searching for convergence points and developing all possible potential for spectacle in order to contribute to the common cause – or rather, the commonality – of world music. The risks of cultural levelling are obvious. Thenceforth, is it necessary to read the writing on the wall and fear the pure and simple disappearance of whole musical traditions, snatched away by this centrifugal force? Fortunately for us, the facts show that this is not necessarily always the case.

But the coexistence of traditional world music and modern world music remains nevertheless problematic because the powers involved are divergent. The first affirms the spiritual identity of established collectivities, whether large civilisations or restricted and culturally fragile communities, while the second extols the fusion of genres and integration at all costs. These two positions are antinomic in essence and any attempt to reconcile them highlights their fundamental antipathy. Is it necessary to sacrifice signs of identity on the altar of integration or to insist on retaining them in the face of exclusion? Many recent events show well that the question applies just as acutely to other domains as it does to the musical sphere; the debate is highly complex, involving multivalent sociological, political and economic stakes whose future interactions are difficult to foresee.

Chapter 9

The Great Bazaar
From the Meeting of Cultures to the
Appropriation of the Exotic

The label *Musiques du Monde* (an approximate translation of the term world music) represents in the French-speaking record industry a multiform musical category of fuzzy and uncertain boundaries. One finds as easily the last supporters of Auvergnat children's rhymes and Parisian *musette* as fans of Central African Pygmy polyphonic yodelling, renowned soloists of Eastern classical traditions, virtuosos of the national folklore of former Eastern Europe and even of the emblematic figures of Congolese *soukous*, Algerian *raï*, Jamaican *raggamuffin*, Andalusian *flamenco*-rock and Indo-Pakistani *bhangra*. In this large souk that is the global village, musical styles which seemed to have nothing in common now overlap, meet, intertwine and sometimes copulate to give birth to unexpected offspring: products of interaction between genres, cultures and technologies.

Just as examples I will cite two random entries from the catalogue of a French importer-distributor of compact discs, both of which are classified under the category world music:

> This live recording of a concert at the Basilica of St Bonifaz in Munich unites for the first time on a single CD Gregorian Christianity, Islam's Sufi music and Jewish temple songs. The spiritual energy of the mystical dialogue of this common plea is transmitted to the listener in an impressive manner resulting from the combination of the three musical styles. The cooperative presence of the three religions, Jewish, Christian and Islamic, beneath the motto *Monotheistischer Dreiklang* (monotheist triad) underlines the unifying element of peoples, cultures and religions.

> They are immigrants from every part of the British Commonwealth – in short, the foreign workers of England. Nearly all members of the group come from immigrant families and carry their cultural background in their music. The music is especially concerned with Indian and Pakistani influences, which are included in the traditional Soul. Jazz influences are also part of the mix and, in JC 001, the group can be proud of a rapper, nominated in the 1993 *Guinness Book of World Records* as the world's fastest rapper.

As we can see, the term's range is broad and its promotional criteria varied. Comfortable, even commanding, the term 'world music' is deeply striking in terms of the heterogeneity that can be extracted from it. In its origin this category of music is assimilated as any simple fashion, nurtured as it is of aesthetic innocence and third-world good feelings, but magnified through the contribution of sophisticated studio technologies; our infatuation for music from elsewhere appears as well in the logic of our multicultural society and its underlying ideology.

Recycling and Normalisation

> I was born in Israel, but I lived there for a short period of time. I travelled quite a lot because I studied folk musics around the world. I studied in California, learned Mexican folk music in Mexico, Indian music in India and African music in Africa. I have assimilated all kinds of traditional techniques in singing and percussion. ... I speak to Europe. I am Slavic, of Russian and Bulgarian origin.

This is how the young singer Meira Asher, now a promising entity in the world of song, defines herself.[1] Her first album, entitled *Dissected*,[2] is noticeable by its provocative, violent and furious texts, exacerbated by music of an intermixed nature where the sounds of the *didgeridoo*, *djembe* or *sitār* vie with those of electronic instruments.

At first sight, world music appears the largest holding pen in the whole of music history. But this domain is not as disorganised as might be imagined, and, after the agitation and ebullience of the beginning of the 1980s,[3] there emerged a period of normalisation of the market which assured the promotion of the genre and its performers. Some believed they were witnessing the musical expression of a deeply altruistic current of thought, of a new frame of mind in which everyone was given the right to speak. Powered by the idea of respect for all, a spontaneous move towards universal fraternity had begun. Others, on the contrary, discovered world music's economic potential and from then on concentrated on developing an image that matched the tastes and expectations of a public by and large young, open and malleable. Indeed, it was soon clear that the economic stakes of the movement hid behind its humanistic surface; it was therefore necessary for record labels to create commercial strategies which recognised these conditions.

In Britain the term world music became widespread in April 1987. Given the lack of a better name, this term was adopted on that date at a meeting of a group of producers and distributors from independent music labels. The nomenclature appears to have been settled via exclusion rather than by deliberate choice since, under the cover of musical diversity, it embraced everything that does not appear in the categories previously available in the music market – namely classical music, rock and pop, jazz and film music. Whatever it is, this symbolic 'act of foundation' equates to an official recognition by professionals. It allowed the institution of what Steven Feld calls 'normative conceptualization' (1995: 101) and therefore permitted

---

1   Meira Asher, cited by Alain Croubalian in his article 'L'écorchée vive Meira Asher' [The live cutaway of Meira Asher], Samedi littéraire of the Journal de Genève and Gazette de Lausanne, 25 January 1997: 37.

2   Meira Asher: Dissected. CD, Crammed Discs, Cram094 (1997).

3   There is no need to rehearse the history of world music here; Denis-Constant Martin (1996a and b) has already proposed an excellent general and critical introduction to the subject.

the cataloguing of world music and its sub-categories according to a certain number of universally applicable criteria and parameters. It was a quickly made thing, and the press contributed by generating such expressions as roots, world beat or world mix which, independently of the ethnic and geocultural origins of the music concerned, have imposed themselves vigorously within the Anglo-Saxon jargon as designations for three world music sub-categories; or, in any case, three dominant tendencies in a market that surges with creolisation.

Roots

According to the *Dico des musiques* (Dictionary of musics), 'the expression designates rural traditional music, rooted music, of the land of origin, and by extension nowadays, the original forms hitherto non-modernised or non-digitalised of a musical genre' (Leduc 1996: 551). This field of application corresponds roughly to that of the terms 'ethnic music(s)' and/or 'traditional music(s)'; it refers to what Constantin Brăiloiu called 'folk music forms which have not undergone any kind of transformation' (cited in Aubert 1985: 43), if such ever existed. The observation rather leads us to note that any music of oral tradition is by definition 'changeable', meaning the changes affecting it are not necessarily of a corruptive nature.

This depiction of roots is thus misleading, as too is the equivalent one of 'sources' used, for example, from the beginning of the 1970s by UNESCO for the disc collection, *Musical Sources*: the idea suggested by these two terms seems to indicate indeed that the genres they define necessarily lead to something other than themselves, that they embody the preliminaries of some posterior development. Obviously, this vision of things does not correspond to reality because the music in question is itself self-sufficient.

World Beat

Also called ethno-pop, this refers to the set of modern music characterised by the predominant use of electric and electronic instruments, mixed, or not, with the timbres of acoustic instruments borrowed from different cultures. For mostly historical reasons related to the music industry's development, European and North American productions of the pop and rock domains are not part of the world beat field because their commercialisation pre-dates it. This category – or at least the majority of what it includes – on the other hand, was born in the West from the collaborations of migrating musicians and European or North American arrangers, sound engineers and producers. The 'raw musical material', particularly the vocal material, is supplied by the former and reworked by the latter, who try to give it a sonority that corresponds to international taste as represented by the latest market trends.

Paris and London played, and continue to play, a pivotal role in the formation and development of certain styles connected to world beat. Well-known showbusiness personalities such as the late George Harrison, Paul Simon, Peter Gabriel, Ry Cooder or Mickey Hart – to mention only the most frequently quoted, although the phenomenon is much vaster – have contributed extensively, and their influence on the careers of certain contemporary Asian, African and Caribbean song stars is well known. Of course, this influence pays them well in return, since it contributes to establishing their image as artists emblematic of anti-racism and active in the dialogue of cultures. Who remembers the names of Joseph Shabalala, leader of Ladysmith Black Mambazo (see Erlmann 1989), or of Steve Mavuso, singer of the Savuka group? On the other hand, those of Paul Simon and Johnny Clegg, the white Zulu, reside in every memory of the heroic fight led in South Africa against apartheid.

But Africa is becoming equipped. 'I wanted to institute a cultural industry in Africa because African culture had not been exploited by the Africans,' affirmed the Guinean singer Mory Kanté.[4] To those that accuse him of having 'lost the soul of his music through contact with pop', Kanté answers:

> When Europeans go to Africa, they disembark with their DAT, record everything they can and mix it with whatever else they wish. It results in discs applauded throughout Europe. But when we, Africans, use this kind of technical perfection, they say we destroy our music. I never disowned anything, I always carried the torch of my cultural identity, I have always sung in Manding, I always played the *kora* and the *balafon*. Europeans have sampled these instruments and everybody adores it. I continue to play them and people call me with contempt the electric griot.[5]

It is true that cities like Dakar, Bamako or Abidjan possess today sophisticated recording studios that begin to vie with those of London or Paris, and these have the great advantage of considerably lower production costs compared to those in Europe. This movement of reappropriation by Africans of the products of their own culture is new and certainly beneficial if one thinks, not only to the world music debut, completely oriented towards the Euro-American market, but also to the immense traffic in 'primitive art' which marked the colonial period. If, for multiple reasons, the repatriation of works remains problematic within the domain of plastic arts, it is, on the other hand, about to become an encouraging and profitable reality in music.

World Mix

This term refers to different intercultural experiences in musical fusion, which consist in mingling timbres, processes and vocal and/or instrumental techniques of various origins. However, this movement must not be confused with the one known as jazz–rock fusion, which was born at the beginning of the 1970s in the United States under the impetus of musicians such as Miles Davis, Larry Coryell and John McLaughlin. Even though the term did not exist at the time, we can already speak about fusion in the sense of world mix when looking at the path of the group Shakti, constituted by the latter with Indian musicians such as L. Shankar, Zakir Hussain and T.S. Vinayakaram; or, ultimately, when looking at George Harrison's career whilst he

---

4   Interview carried out by Radio Suisse Romande on 22 January 1997, on the release of his CD, *Tatebola*, Misslin DME 18 (1997).

5   Mory Kanté, cited by Vicent Borcard in the article 'Les vérités de Mory Kanté' [The Truths of Mory Kanté], *Le Matin* (Lucerne), 26 January 1997: 47.

composed pieces like 'Love You To' for the Beatles' disc *Revolver* (1966) or 'Within You, Without You' for the cult album *Sergeant Pepper's Lonely Hearts Club Band* (1967);[6] or even when looking at jazzmen such as Don Cherry, Yussef Lateef and Clifford Thornton, who, at the same time, looked to African or Asian instrumentaria for the timbres of an alternative music with great political connotation. Within the folk music revival sphere at the end of the 1960s we can mention a group called The Incredible String Band, whose display of Orientalism largely contributed to its popularity.

A much more spectacular example of *mix* is provided by the music of Martin Scorsese's controversial film *The Last Temptation of Christ* (1989),[7] concocted by Peter Gabriel in his Real World studios. Entitled *Passion*, the main part of this soundtrack is a programme in itself, uniting such varied musicians as the late, great Pakistani *qawwāl* Nusrat Fateh Ali Khan, the Senegalese griot Youssou N'Dour and the British countertenor Julian Wilkins, with instrumentalists including the trumpeter John Hassel (USA), L. Shankar (India) on electric violin, the Brazilian percussionist Djalma Correa and Peter Gabriel himself on synthesizers and sampler. It is necessary to underline that this project involved the total consent of each participant and that they were paid normally for their contribution as studio musicians.

The development of sampler capacities increased considerably the expressive range and commercial potential of this genre. Sampling, which consists in borrowing a sample of a prerecorded music and replicating it – just as it is or electronically reprocessed – obviously allows every kind of manipulation: Mory Kanté made allusion to this, which poses serious ethical problems, in particular with regard to the division of authors' rights and interpreters' royalties.

The practice is spreading and has already caused numerous polemics that have ended up in the courtrooms. The Turkish musician Kudsi Erguner relates, for example, that in 1989 he discovered with astonishment an excerpt of one of his improvisations (*taksīm*) on *ney* flute in *Revolutions* by Jean-Michel Jarre (1988),[8] a work commissioned and composed for festivities celebrating the French Revolution's bicentenary. Jarre had indeed acquired from the sound engineer, Xavier Bellenger, an unpublished recording of Erguner, produced at Senanque Abbey (the narrative does not say under exactly what conditions). An excerpt of this recording had then been 'reworked' and harnessed by Jarre, using current sampling techniques. The file for the prosecution instituted by Erguner on Jarre revealed that in 18 months Jarre had received 690,000 French francs as rights for the composition: none of this had been paid to Erguner, who was not even credited on the cover of the CD in question. The judicial confrontation turned to Erguner's advantage but resulted in his receiving a modest indemnity, which did not even cover his lawyer's expenses.[9]

---

6   For an analysis of Hindustani influence in the Beatles' music, see Leante 2000.

7   Peter Gabriel: Passion: Music for the Last Temptation of Christ of Martin Scorsese. CD, Real World RWCD2 (1989).

8   Jean-Michel Jarre: Revolutions. CD Dreyfus-Polygram 837421-2 PY 900 (1988).

9   As told by Kudsi Erguner. We can also find the narration of it in his autobiography (Erguner 2000: 144–5), published after this chapter was written.

This anecdote is suggestive of a new kind of musical plagiarism that is spreading, and whose abuses have begun to be denounced. An important ethnomusicological journal, the *Yearbook for Traditional Music*, dedicated the major part of a volume to these kinds of questions. It notably refers to the famous album *Deep Forest*,[10] whose extraordinary success constitutes a spectacular example – in any case, with regard to its economic consequences: it sold about 2.5 million copies in four years. The two introductory contributions to this volume (Feld 1996 and Zemp 1996) provide some edifying information on the nature of the processes involved in this kind of musico-mercantile fiddling around – processes they condemn straightforwardly. Offering stupendous descriptions of the different manipulations that can affect music like that of the BaBenzélé Pygmies of Central Africa once it is published on disc, Feld's article introduces the disturbing expression 'schizophonic mimesis', whose definition appears progressively throughout the pages and processes described by the author. Here are some of the terms he uses on the subject, listed in alphabetic order, to avoid any hierarchising temptation:

> adaptation, appropriation, artistic dialogue, artistic transformation, caricatured picture, celebration, circulation, cooperation, disjunction, global apparatus, hybridism, imitation, inspiration, manipulation, post-colonial devastation, purely primitivist fantasy, recycling, referenciality, reminiscent, social altruism, subrogation, technocrat attitude …

Where to find a better catalogue of the mechanisms involved in the tendency to *mix* world music?

There are also a number of more-or-less unclassifiable musical trajectories, which do not enter any of these three sub-categories but still partake of the general world music movement. Leduc signals the emergence at the end of 1995 of the term transmusic, which he defines as: 'At the same time "trance music" and "transversal music", this music crosses the musical and mental barriers to look for ecstasy, the true feeling that surpasses everything' (1996: 636). Ideologically very close to the New Age neo-spiritualist movement, this current appears as a space with potential for the accomplishment of any kind of fantasy and for personal journeys of varied natures and interests.

Sometimes frankly commercial, sometimes tinted with good feelings, or even purely empirical, instances of this music are too varied for us to be able to offer a global overview of them; but we can look at the implications of one such music, namely that which is called 'harmonic' or 'overtone' singing. Developed and originated within traditions of Central Asia – in particular in the music of Mongolia, Tuva and, on a smaller scale, of Tibet – this technique consists in privileging in vocal emission one or another harmonic of the sound spectrum in parallel with the fundamental tone. Signalled since the beginning of the twentieth century by inspired missionary writings such as those of Father van Oost (1915), this musical phenomenon attracted the attention of various ethnomusicologists, whose publications have fascinated curious minds. The discovery that this technique resulted from the application of a method, of a rather simple 'means', and that we had every possibility of learning

---

10 The protagonists of *Deep Forest* chose the term 'world mix' as the subtitle of their album, *Deep Forest: World Mix*. CD Columbia 476589-2 (1994).

overtone singing ourselves, has induced applied research by individuals and by groups of adepts. Several ensembles in different locations have sprung up, devoted to the practice of 'renovated' overtone singing and regularly organising training courses.

Three musicians with very distinct trajectories, each of whom enjoys a certain degree of popularity, integrate this technique into their vocal practice: one among them is the French singer and mathematician of Russian origin Iegor Reznikoff, whose research in the domain of 'fundamental liturgy' based on the interpretation of Gregorian and pre-Gregorian plainchant has been greatly influenced by the discovery of these vocal techniques.[11] Regarding this matter, Reznikoff's liner notes talk of 'psychophysiological states and of sounding resonance of the body, characteristic of these states Antiquity used to call *movements of the soul*'.

The Parisian Vietnamese Tran Quang Hai is a second performer of overtone singing. As well as being a musician, he is also a versatile ethnomusicologist connected to the Musée de l'Homme and is interested in the spectral analysis of overtone singing explored through his own vocal practice (see for example Zemp and Tran 1991). As for the New Yorker David Hykes, since 1975 he and his ensemble, the Harmonic Choir, have devoted themselves to a systematic exploration of the unexploited resources of these vocal processes, as he says, 'so that overtone singing can serve what seems to me to be its main goal: to become a kind of "global sacred music" for the modern times'.[12]

Is this a case of transmusic, or merely experimental world music? It is difficult to say; but what we can reveal is that shortly after David Hykes's CD release *A l'écoute des vents solaires/Hearing Solar Winds* for the collection Ocora/Radio France,[13] which is dedicated to 'traditional' music of the world, Pierre Toureille, then the collection's director, recognised that although this disc did not truly fit the collection, its sales had beaten all records and therefore would permit the financing of many upcoming issues in the collection.[14]

The Evolution of a Market

A category without satisfactory definition, world music has become an enormous commercial arena for the music industry. Almost 300,000 titles are currently available on the European market, to which about 10,000 new items are added every year. In 1996, the world music section of the market in France represented more than 12 per cent of in-store sales, equating to double the sales of jazz – including blues, gospel and soul (6 per cent) – and practically as much as classical music from the Middle Ages to the contemporary period (14 per cent); meanwhile, French song sold 20 per

---

11   Listen, for example, to his album *Le Chant de Fontenay. Liturgie fondamentale et grand chant de soliste grégorien.* CD SM 1216.40 (1989).

12   Interview with the author on Radio Suisse Romande, Résonances, broadcast on 14 April 1991.

13   David Hykes: A l'écoute de vents solaires/Hearing Solar Winds. CD Ocora C 558607 (1987).

14   Oral presentation by Pierre Toureille.

cent, international pop and rock 30 per cent and, finally, the sector grouping music video and film music 18 per cent.

A study of FNAC outlets in Paris revealed that the section 'musics of the world' of this large enterprise – one of the most important in Europe – sold about 230,000 CDs from January to October 1996. This allows us to estimate annual sales as close to 300,000 discs, considering the seasonal increase of business in the run-up to New Year's Eve parties. In percentages these sales were geoculturally distributed in the following way:

Antilles, Réunion, *salsa*	26.8%
Europe	18.6%
Sub-Saharan Africa	16.6%
Reggae, ragga and ragamuffin	14.3%
Latin America	8.6%
Orient (North Africa and Near Orient), including *raï*	8.6%
Asia	3.9%
Various (Oceania, North America, compilations)	2.6%[15]

Constantly monitoring the evolution of the national and world market, promoters of this kind of music note the existence (independent of the main fashion trends) of a flux phenomenon which is sometimes very temporary, linked to events, tours, media 'kick-off's' and, generally, to the influence of the press. Caribbean and African pop represent the vast majority of world music sales – a total of 57.7 per cent – and it is thanks to this that these promoters say they are also able to take care 'of the rest', and especially of marginal specialised catalogues of 'ethnic and traditional' music. This observation can soothe the consciences of those for whom the large world music market seems only an ominous threat to the survival of cultural heritage and regional musical identities. As Hugo Zemp (1996: 36) rightly says, 'more and more, ethnomusicological research and commercial exploitation are getting intertwined'; this interdependence appears above all to have economic terms.

The record dealers in question are anxious to underline the important proportion of immigrants among their clientele: 'This musical section would not exist as such without the presence of immigrants, African in particular, in Paris.' African song now seems to be going through a slight deviation; its performers are turning today more towards styles such as *ska* and *rap*.[16] Whatever the situation, it is interesting to note that African traditional music represents a nearly insignificant business category: Africans from Paris do not identify themselves with it and often do not appreciate the idea of an 'ethnic disc', which they would tend to perceive as a kind of

---

15   The presence of generic determinants mingled with others, indicating regions, is explained by the fact that the production of *salsa* is not confined to Cuba and Puerto Rico, any more than *reggae* and its derivatives is to Jamaica and *raï* to Algeria; rather these genres developed considerably within corresponding diasporas, *salsa* mainly in the United States, *reggae* in the UK and *raï* in France.

16   Because of its North American origin, in record shops English- and French-language *rap* is situated in the section for rock and its derivatives, and not in 'world music'.

cultural neocolonialism. Admirers of these more 'authentic' genres, including stars such as the very modern Malian female griot Oumou Sangaré, are usually white. Africans seem to appreciate music for its danceability, whereas Europeans prefer to buy African music to listen to.

The concept of 'traditional' music is not – or, is no longer – a distinctive criterion applied for ordering discs. Already in numerous regions of the world it appears that tradition is no longer popular, or even no longer exists. Evidently, it is not the record dealers' duty to determine, for example, what is and what is not traditional in a given musical culture. It is, on the other hand, their role to make choices according to the demands of the market. Regarding the Asian domain, Parisian audiences are not generally interested in contemporary pop music and therefore this is practically absent from the shelves; but traditional music of Asia, and in particular its scholarly genres, have a faithful and constant audience who justify a regular updating of the publishers' catalogues. As for the European domain, it is currently increasing because of two recent waves: the renewal of 'Celtic' Breton, especially Irish music, and the Gypsy music of Eastern European countries. We should also point out that among the European popular genres Italian song appears in the '*variété*, song' section of records shops, music from Greece within 'world music' and that from Germany nowhere: 'pure pragmatism', they affirm!

In contrast, one Parisian record dealer who did specialise in the music of the world, 'from ethnic to world music, passing through folklore, folk and trad', took the liberty a few years ago of displaying the recordings according to his personal preferences.[17] There was no reggae or *raï* there but, and on the other hand, there was practically everything that existed on European 'trad' music,[18] in particular French and Irish, as well as accordion music in all its possible latitudes and different shapes. The reasons for this choice were essentially bound to an apparent soft spot for those genres within the boss's personal taste. With a stock of about 5,000 titles, he had made an assessment of his clientele, which he broke down in the following way:

- one-third 'European trad' enthusiasts, with Celtic music at the top, representing 50 per cent of sales, currently increased by music of Eastern European Gypsies;
- one-third 'regulars' attracted by the unusual – Mongolian overtone singing, Inuit throat games, Yakut rock, Pygmy yodelling, Zulu concertina and, especially, Australian didgeridoo, of which he sold about 200 discs per month;
- one-third 'Mr and Mrs Everybody' (passers-by, locals, tourists coming back from Bali, stressed businesspeople in search of music for relaxation …), of highly fluctuating tastes.

---

17   5 Planètes. 10 rue Saint-Sébastien, 75011 Paris. (This store no longer exists.)

18   The term 'trad' is not merely the diminutive of 'traditional'; it entered the current language of French performers in parallel with the creation of *Trad Magazine*, geared to a genre that descended from folk music. Those involved have renounced the eclecticism of the 1960s and 70s and instead 'concentrate on music, style and instruments of only one region, with the intention to make them evolve.'

This analysis is not, however, representative of the clientele for 'musics of the world' discs; contrary to the case at FNAC, for example, immigrants were imperceptible because of their lack of proximity and, above all, because the genres that attracted them were not for sale there. Nevertheless the existence of a small enterprise of this type is already in itself a sign of evolution.

In the same category there is a store in Geneva that opened in the late 1960s and was at the time exclusively dedicated to jazz discs. Gradually, from the beginning of 1980s it became devoted 'to all musics "of the world" – which doesn't mean to all musics from around the world.'[19] The shop offers close to 10,000 titles: about half from the jazz, blues and funk sectors, and the other half all kinds of music from around the world. There, we also find at the heart of this specialised trade the boss's passion, which has essentially moved towards 'authentic' musics, a phrase he insists in pronouncing with its attendant quotation marks by using a different tone of voice.

World music continues to take off, he noted. More and more, the young search for alternatives to the artificial, virtual and hypocritical world offered by current commercial productions, which results in their turning towards the traditional sources of the styles they customarily listen to. After the take-off of West African modern music, the Manding griots attracted a much larger audience, for example; and, as for the Cuban domain, the old *son* masters just as popular as contemporary *salsa* stars (a trend that has nothing to do with the situation in Cuba, where only the most strident music captures the attention of the public at large).

Regarding New Age music, this record dealer admits his aversion to the genre; when customers are searching for 'mind-blowing' music, he prefers to direct them to Oriental traditional styles – and especially to music from India – affirming that 'a good Hariprasad Chaurasia disc does the job just as well and, in addition, it's sublime and not dangerous!'

The Trivialisation of the Exotic

The abundance of published discs has without doubt opened the public's appreciation to numerous unexpected genres. Unknown musical traditions have been brought to our knowledge thanks to remarkable recordings made by exacting professionals, anxious to select what appeared to them the best and most representative musical worlds – worlds which we never previously suspected in terms of beauty, significance or even existence.

Some specialist publishers dedicate themselves to this domain with expertise and discernment; others, mostly concerned with the mass market, make occasional incursions according to the economic potential that such–and–such a fashionable genre or famous artist represents. But these are rare exceptions, and most recordings only have an insignificant financial impact on the market, and therefore on the owners; or rather on the performers of the genres in question. It is always useful to proclaim that a part of the royalties and other profits from such-and-such a disc

---

19 Disco-Club, 22 rue des Terreaux-du-Temple, 1201 Geneva.

has been given to the community of origin, and that a copy of the recording has been scrupulously restored to them or, if they do not have the means to use it, that it has been transferred to a local expert or representative institution. But it is obvious that none of these charitable gestures can in itself provide more than a part of the solution to the real difficulties confronted by these traditions, their holders and the cultures from which they emerge. The result is that some genres stay practically unknown, others die out after being well documented by researchers – who did not have the means to save them – and others find unexpected public success without their performers and even, to a smaller extent, the ethnomusicologists to whom we owe the 'discovery', being there very much.

More than a simple trend, the taste – or even the infatuation, in certain cases – for music of the world became therefore a genuine mass phenomenon of simultaneously musical and social impact. On the musical plane, the most modern of these genres attract today a large part of the audiences for rock, folk and Western (especially Anglo-Saxon) popular music, whose creativity seems to have run out of steam for some years now. Other genres, on the contrary, attract the public through the sophistication and depth of their expressive tradition, representing in that respect a current comparable to that of European early music. Others, still, surprise with their unexpected aesthetics, timbres and extraordinary techniques. In their entirety, these genres seem to affirm a set of alternative and regenerative directions that stand in opposition to those of other present musical trends.

Nevertheless the social dimension of world music is just as important. We know the success experienced by the 'mega concerts' broadcast universally in the 1980s, such as *Live Aid*, *Tribute to Mandela* and *We Are the World* (Martin 1996b: 4–6). Assembled by rock stars with the collusion of musicians 'of the world' (mainly African), these events – which followed the lineage of festivals like those organised at Woodstock, Monterey or the Isle of Man since the late 1960s – created in today's youth a feeling more of interethnic than intercultural solidarity, whose effects are increasingly manifest. The awarding, during *Victoires de la Musique 1997*, of the trophy for 'best French song of the year' to 'Aïcha' – composed by Jean-Jacques Goldman and sung by the *raï* star Khaled – is a striking example, especially as it has obviously been influenced equally by political and artistic factors.

In a deeper way, this solidarity implies that the listening of the other is different, insofar as we recognise that he or she is a holder of values we have lost, or even never known. That is probably the highest form of exoticism, as Victor Segalen claimed when he wrote in 1911 in his *Essai sur l'exotisme*: 'My faculty to feel the Diverse and recognise its beauty, drives me to hate all those that attempt to weaken (in their ideas or forms) or deny it, by building boring synthesis' (1995: 34). His fear of 'Diverse insipidness' (ibid.: 80) addresses well the various kinds of reticence prevailing in the 'fusion' trend within world music, characterising this music as a standardised and homogenised expression in which all asperities have been erased to form the famous soft consensus generated by the Audimat god cult. The music genres of the world have certainly acquired merchant values; but they remain above all human values, in the noblest sense of the term. Their appearance in our immediate environment returns to us today an echo of the society we live in: a society in crisis, questioning its foundations due to the recent eruption of plurality; but especially a society in mutation, facing the emergency of redefining its ethics through reference to a new set of solicitations of which our society is the object.

The margin is narrow between, on one hand, the pure and simple dismissal of all kinds of arbitrary hybridisation in the name of the preservation of the separate identity of each tradition, and, on the other, the fraternal glorification of the intercultural at all costs. Nostalgia for an alleged purity of cultures – which recalls a little too much of the fascist ideology of the 'purity of races' – is in this respect as pernicious as the globalist Utopia of the fusion of cultures. The diverse has lost the aura of exoticism that fascinated Segalen; today, constituent of our society and its culture, diversity has become a major stake in political confrontation; but it is, at the same time, a vital ferment in the renewal of our creativity.

Chapter 10

Learning the Music of the Other
A Transcultural Itinerary

Integration and Institutionalisation: a Second Breath?

For some years now, certain Western vocational musical and educational institutions have come to play an important role in the propagation of the world's musical traditions by teaching pupils either born or living outside the original context of these genres. Initially, this practice was experimental and marginal, but it has now achieved a hitherto unexpected prominence. After some North American universities introduced the practical study of world music into ethnomusicological programmes of study – here the pioneering work in this area by Ki Mantle Hood at the University of California in Los Angeles deserves to be signalled (see Hood 1960: 55–9) – a certain number of conservatories and music schools, particularly in Europe, created departments dedicated to the teaching of 'musics of the world'. Other institutes and associations arose that were dedicated exclusively to these genres, or to one amongst them. Since 1992, an international conference has been organised annually on the theme of the integration of extra-European music into academic programmes of education and musical training (see Schippers 1992 and Lieth-Philipp and Gutzwiller 1995).

This practice raises certain questions considered here. The first concern in the argument, often a foregone conclusion, is that it is necessary to be born into a culture to be able to master its music. This assertion is obviously false – it is necessary to insist on this – insofar as musical knowledge is not in any case a genetic particularity; in an obvious way, it results entirely from the domain of cultural acquisition. The only innate faculty in this respect is the propensity we can call talent or musical gift, which is only a greater or lesser degree of ease in seizing the product of an experience and in exploiting its potential according to the conventions it activates. If a musician from East Asia can become a fully licensed interpreter of European classical music – and there are many cases to show this – then the converse is necessarily true also; and again there are several examples to prove it.[1]

It is correct that the training in a foreign music will remain necessarily limited if it is not matched with a good knowledge of its context, and possibly its language or one of its operative languages. In addition, the pupil's determination must be strong

---

1   The festival *Résonances: musiciens d'ici – musiques d'ailleurs* [Resonances: musicians from here – music from elsewhere] organised in Geneva in 1982, 1985, 1987, 1989 and 1991 by the Ateliers d'ethnomusicologie took as its goal the illustration of the phenomenon of 'transculturality' by presenting many musicians representative of this trend.

because, as compared to a native schoolmate, he or she has a priori the handicap of having to become familiar with musical aesthetics that are initially quite unfamiliar. The hazards, especially those of a psychological order, are real and numerous, particularly due to differences in ways of thinking. Partial teaching, badly discerned or perceived, may provoke a rejection, or even problems such as the emergence of a schizophrenic personality type, where a student is motivated at home but fragile or insufficiently prepared for further contact and, above all, lacks a sense of identification with the sociocultural group that normally possesses the knowledge.

It is therefore right to replicate as far as possible the pre-existing conditions of transmission of every type of music or, at least, to respect their coherence and adapt their methods with discernment. There is such a diversity of music teaching methods in the world that no model is universally applicable. From the more precise and systematic ones to those based on no obvious formalisation, each suits its musical sphere and the way of life that accompanies it. The role and function of a genre determines to a large measure its mode of acquisition; these are important criteria which need to be taken into account when considering the dissemination of musical practices outside their original cultural environments.

Certain types of music are shared by a whole collectivity and, from childhood, every individual is immersed in a milieu of which these are an indisoluble element. Musical training is not the object of any explicit plan; it takes place through progressive impregnation as naturally as spoken language. In the absence of this context an immersion approach is not possible unless a judicious pedagogy and group dynamic can restore its ambience and synthesise the essential information.

In this respect, the example of Bali is a striking one: from a very young age every boy begins his musical training by letting a metallophone's sound penetrate his ears, often while he is asleep in his father's lap as the latter rehearses with the village *gamelan*. As he grows, the child starts playing the easiest instruments, the large gongs, which he has to hit at the end of every cycle – once every eight or sixteen beats; he will then be assigned more and more complex parts and instruments to play, this happening progressively according to his ability. His training is considered finished when he shows himself capable of mastering every instrument in the orchestra and can play its part in the ensemble. The roles are in fact perfectly interchangeable between members of a Balinese *gamelan*, even though some specialise in playing the set of metallophones, the flute or the drum.

Other musical genres are exclusive to determined social categories – castes or lineages, age or gender groups, professional ensembles and so on – outside of which their performance is in principle forbidden, or at least judged as incongruous; it is evidently the case with such music that its acquisition by a stranger risks presenting more problems, because in principle such a person is not qualified to gain access to it. The contemporary situation often questions these statutes of limitation, but they remain solidly anchored in traditional mentalities, so much are they linked to a network of beliefs and customs that justifies the existence of these genres and that determines their modes of playing. Here, appropriation by foreigners may sometimes be perceived negatively by the music's accustomed holders.

Among 'reserved' genres, there are those which are only played on certain occasions, in the absence of which they lose any meaning; here, it is the nature of the occasion that establishes whether the export of its musical component is well founded, or even possible at all. It is obvious that ceremonial music, belonging to a ritual complex and including a sacred dimension, requires deep circumspection because it puts into action energies whose influence and management the stranger often ignores. Other genres, for example lullabies, festivity music or work songs, normally do not raise these kinds of problems, although they still contain in essence a normative and prophylactic virtue.

The category better adapted to integration in a foreign institutional setting is probably that of music of a voluntary nature, within which no principle of restriction opposes its diffusion. These are genres generally suitable for interpretation in a concert and therefore for export and, in fact, are those that recruit more adepts from different cultures. We can roughly distinguish two subcategories, the first being so-called art music; like European classical music, it includes an explicit theory and time-tested teaching methods. The great art traditions of the East – such as *rāga* in the Indian subcontinent and *maqām* throughout the Arabian world, Turkey, Iran, Azerbaijan and Central Asia – are obviously part of it, as is chamber and court music of East Asia; but one can also include African court music and other musical genres traditionally linked to serving an elite. As with European classical music, these forms became very widely disseminated outside their initial borders, sometimes even all over the world, which allowed many amongst them to survive the decay and disappearance – today almost universal – of their initial milieu.

Other genres with equal degrees of sophistication have remained the prerogative of restricted circles of adepts; in principle, they are not intended to be played in public because their intimate nature is itself inimical to it. These genres rehearse, in the best sense of the term, answers to concerns of a philosophical and religious order, and access to some of them may even require a formal initiation, without which contact remains only partial and superficial. These kind of practices can be found in most Oriental spiritual traditions: among these we can mention the link between Chinese Confucianism and the *qin* zither, Zen Buddhism of Japan and the *shakuhachi* flute, Sufism, to which are connected the art of the *setār* lute in Iran and the *ney* flute in various Middle Eastern countries, or even some Hindu schools in which the practice of music is considered as a form of yoga. Meditation methods par excellence, these music genres are simultaneously techniques and demonstrations of subtle alchemical processes: while cultivating the art of sounds, the insider in a certain way makes the silence manifest itself, while trying to control the impulses of his or her ego; through the virtues of discipline performers harmonise their inner state with the cosmic order, progressing thus onto a path of wisdom and detachment. Access to these practices requires a particular disposition which, in itself, relies less on a specific cultural investment than on the personal aspirations of the incoming learner. In all, nothing opposes access to these music-related experiences if the master respects the setting and the disciple is endowed with the required qualifications.[2]

Music of popular tradition also awakens the interest of young foreigners. Its often communal dimension contributes to its appeal, the reasons for which may be either social or merely musical. While participating in a collective practice of a festive

---

2   On this subject see, Goormaghtigh 1990.

nature, pupils satisfy a legitimate hunger for sharing and celebration, a desire which may have been frustrated in their own cultural context, including its modern popular music. Among these one can mention, for example, Andean flutes, African or Afro-American percussion, or even certain forms of Indonesian *gamelan* as mentioned above; all have relatively significant numbers of Western adepts.

It is still necessary to note that vocal genres are a lot more difficult to approach than their instrumental counterparts. The reasons for this are linguistic handicaps; and then the fact that the voice is in a way an 'essential instrument' which requires the student's total investment in the musical aesthetics of his or her choice. Timbre is also a central matter because, in contrast to the instrumentalist, the singer uses his or her own voice and the cultural determination of vocal intonation is extremely strong.

In general, excepting its technical difficulties, access to music 'from elsewhere' also requires overcoming difficulties placed by our own aesthetic and psychological conditioning: a non-tempered melodic scale, an asymmetric rhythm or an unusual sound production technique can, indeed, cause a kind of barrier that is not always easy to overcome. To be efficient, the teaching of these processes requires a 'pedagogic strategy' adapted to the handicaps formed by the pupil's previous experience; we must consider his or her musical past null and void and 'start with a blank slate' in any case.

The Principles of Orality

One of the general features of traditional music is the orality of its transmission. Those genres that make systematic or occasional recourse to written aids do not question the common principle of orality: this is even the case in scholarly or ritual repertoires, in which interpreters must respect the rules rigorously. Certain musical genres belonging to this category, such as the vocal and instrumental classical works of Southern India, Tibetan ritual chant and some of the art repertoire of East Asia, use types of notations which are either neumatic – comparable to that of European medieval plainchant – or ideographic, especially in the form of instrumental tablatures.

Investigations have generally demonstrated that these notations are mostly posterior to the creation of the works they transcribe, as attested to in the observable variants of one manuscript in relation to another; we are not dealing with scores, in the sense given by Western classical musicians to the term, because they only provide the essential elements of a composition and not its exact contour. It is often the case, for example, that the indications relating to rhythm and ornamentation are not even present at all. These notations are descriptive and indicative, not prescriptive; they are essentially a reminder, whose role is to extend and reinforce the effects of the master's direct transmission to the pupil, and in no way to substitute for it.

Recent music transcriptions coming from traditions in decline are generally written according to the Western conventional system, and can be placed in a similar category insofar as they are above all destined to be a recollection of the music in case the oral tradition fails. The survival of a genre such as the Ottoman *fasıl*, which was banned in the Kemalist epoch, is thus largely owed to the works of Turkish musicologists at the end of the nineteenth and the first half of the twentieth centuries; but, given the academicism that blights most contemporary interpretations – at least in their 'official' versions – we can see that having the writing as an exclusive recourse is not sufficient to preserve all the flavour and fluidity of an aesthetics so intimately connected with principles of an oral tradition.[3]

Therefore, it is important when opening music schools specialising in the arts of other cultures to take into account the crucial necessities of each tradition, without wanting to make them correspond to a canvas of over-restrictive regulations and inappropriate educational principles. The use of a notation system based on pentagrams for teaching a genre that traditionally ignores notation is thus not justifiable, even when modified according to the melodic and rhythmic details of the music under consideration. The use of special signs to indicate intervals smaller than a semitone and the transcription of 'limping' rhythms in uneven periodicities by way of conventionally metered bars are useful analytic means; but they do not lead to satisfactory results in teaching because they undermine the educational principles and pedagogic tools characteristic of those genres.

Among the specifically modern auxiliary processes, the sound or video recording of a lesson or its summary is, in this respect, distinctly preferable because it is a direct extension of oral teaching; reviewing in it allows for close listening and, in the long term, it constitutes a precious reservoir of information.[4] However, the use of this working aid also can introduce a threat when pushed to extremes: musicians may become excellent imitators when they copy systematically a great master's improvisations, but their playing will likely remain completely devoid of individual inspiration. From the beginning of the 1970s, the success of a musician such as Ravi Shankar, for example, pushed innumerable young Indian *sitār* players to plan their playing according to his; but these carbon copies hardly have artistic interest, no more than might a good reproduction of the *Mona Lisa*. A music interpretation implies, to some degree, the practice of variation or improvisation, which is necessarily an autonomous act. When a singer's or an instrumentalist's purpose is to replicate slavishly the art of another, he or she misses the target, and his or her trajectory will necessarily lead to a dead end because it flagrantly contradicts the eminently creative aspect of the music that he or she is trying to reproduce.

---

3   However, we can point out the trajectory, exemplary for more than one reason, of a musician like Kudsi Erguner, which has contributed to restoring 'historical truth' to this music's present expression.

4   The sound or audiovisual recording plays an important role in the preservation of a threatened musical repertoire. Significant ethnomusicologist's systematic collections, or 'complete' publications, include that of Moroccan *nūbāt* published by the Paris Maison des cultures du monde with the aid of the Moroccan Ministry of Culture (72 CDs Inédit) and the Persian *radif* as performed by the Iranian musician Dariush Tāla'i (5 CDs Al Sur ALCD 116-20, 1994).

The Choice of a Master

Even on the ethical plane alone, the opening of our conservatories and music schools to cultural plurality is highly desirable. But such an opening must necessarily rest on the set of criteria already evoked, lest it otherwise slides towards a new kind of cultural colonialism. The encouraging accomplishments of several European institutions in this domain can be used as models, each of them forming a point of repose from which we can note the experiences gained so far and, in certain instances, adjust the overall aims. The selection of teachers is, for example, fundamental – even more than for the music of written traditions – because they must possess at the same time an ample knowledge of their art and particular talent in terms of how to transmit it to motivated, if not necessarily well-prepared, pupils.

Even when artistically highly qualified, a recently disembarked master risks slipping up due to an insufficient knowledge of Western attitudes and living conditions. The problem of students' available time, even that of the most determined, presents itself, for example, in completely different terms in European or North American cities as compared to the usual environments of most of these music genres, in particular those of rural origin. Therefore, the master needs to synthesise and condense the teaching while selecting essential data from the education he or she has received, without insisting too much on the more anecdotal and contingent aspects.

Inversely, the artist who has left his or her country for a very long time may tend to adjust systematically to the psychology of his or her pupils. This artist will only show them what he or she knows or believes best corresponds to their expectations or abilities in the domain. Because of prolonged distance, he or she might forget or only partially remember certain important components of the musical knowledge, or even lose contact with the milieu and paramusical realities normally inseparable from vocal or instrumental practice. Respect for the contingencies of performance must be part of the musical apprenticeship, or serious mistakes in comprehension will arise. Nevertheless, sometimes distance allows the master to form a kind of 'panoramic view' of his or her own culture, a more synthetic view, or an 'academic distance' that is actually helpful to the clearer discernment of musical details.

Sometimes emigration causes an astonishing conservatism, a resistance to change, thanks to which whole repertoires forgotten for a long time in their regions of origin have been maintained intact among migrant communities. A well-known case is the folk songs of the French provinces of the seventeenth and eighteenth centuries, long forgotten in France but still alive in Quebec and Louisiana. There are, as a further example, a certain number of musical genres among the Indian community of Trinidad, in particular seasonal chants connected to agricultural rituals, which are today extinct in India but have been preserved intact in the Caribbean.[5]

A third type of teacher is represented by those who were themselves born outside the culture whose music they play. Their own previous path constitutes a substantial educational asset; having already made the intellectual effort to succeed at an a priori exotic musical knowledge, they often view this achievement in a manner that is lucid,

---

5   Personal communication by Laxmi B. Tewari.

global and comparative with reference to its methods of acquisition. It is obviously important that they have received a complete training, certified by their own masters or by the most esteemed bearers of the tradition in question, and that they respect its canons. But, except the inconvenience it can represent for certain pupils who worry that their master does not 'look right for the job', no objection of principle should oppose such a teacher's activity.

The Conditions of Apprenticeship

Whatever the personality and origin of the music master, his or her role is to attract the attention of the pupils to the criteria of excellence of a musical idiom and the particularities of its expression. An apprenticeship in certain genres is extremely arduous and requires many years' experience and daily practice. India, for example teems with stories that attest to the asceticism musical training requires. We ascribe to the *sarod* master Alauddin Khan the story of a child whose father forced him to practise for 16 hours a day. To prevent his son from falling asleep while at work, a tuft of his hair was attached to one end of a rope, and the other end was tied to a hook fixed on the ceiling of the practise room. So, every time he dozed off, the young musician was instantaneously awakened by the pain. To ease his torment, the musician would regularly break a string of his instrument so that he could stop and rest his bruised fingers for the amount of time needed to replace the string.

Other music genres can only be played in a group, and regular collective practice is indispensable for their assimilation. But all are coherent languages which apply musical grammar and syntax, the rules of which must be mastered by the apprentice when acquiring the basics of performance skills.

In this respect, the principle of bi-musicality recommended by Ki Mantle Hood (1960) – it would be preferable to call it 'musical bilingualism', insofar as musicality is a general quality – is certainly useful in the academic study of music because it allows the student of ethnomusicology to penetrate to the heart of his or her topic and to be sensitised to the aesthetic, technical and, to a certain extent, relational aspects of the music towards which the research is oriented. But, if the pupil's main goal is the personal acquisition of a musical language, it is preferable that she or he abandons all comparative concerns, and even all other musical practices, at least temporarily, concentrating exclusively on his or her objective. In the long run, recourse to external references can only preclude progression and distract from direct perception of the musical universe the pupil has decided to enter. The pupil needs to be able to leave behind his or her cultural conditioning or, at least, to succeed in modifying it – not only mentally, but also at the level of sensitivity. A prior overly advanced musical schooling presents more inconveniences than advantages because it implies habits often anchored in the deepest conscience: for example, musical reading, which can result in an inability to conceive a melody unless it is seen as a series of notes written on a score.

The reproduction of intervals different from those to which the subject has become accustomed can also present a serious handicap when accessing a new musical universe. This subject reminds me of a meeting between an Iraqi singer and an Italian singer trained in European early music and therefore, in principle, accustomed to problems of intonation and intervallic precision, especially when interpreting the medieval repertoire. The latter was, however – despite her good will – incapable of reproducing with accuracy the smallest Oriental musical phrase, even though she clearly discerned its melodic finesse, so much was her ear conditioned by the European division of the octave into 12 semitones. Reciprocally, the Iraqi had all the difficulties in the world imitating the nuances of baroque vibrato, the glottal work it implied being completely foreign to her.

From a certain level of exigency, an apprenticeship in music taken outside its original context faces limits related to the gulf separating this music from the student's immediate environment, and because of the risks of distortion that follow from this. If the student does not have the chance to become established in the music's country of origin, it is important that he or she can pay prolonged or frequent visits there. To understand the essence of the music, the student must become immersed in its ambience, the customs that surround it and the meanings the music has for its habitual users. Frequenting the same places as qualified traditional masters will contribute to the development of a favourable mimetic process for the assimilation of aesthetic nuances and the socio- or ethnopsychological implications of the musical expression in question. Indeed, this maintains an organic relation between the music and the milieu, each of which testifies to the stylistic particularities of the other.

All musical architectonics include norms relative to their components, such as timbre, metre, consonance, precision of intervals and intonation, and clarity of articulation. Once assimilated, these elements must be measured according to objective criteria – related to valid aesthetic conceptions in the description of a culture – as well as subjective criteria relevant to the taste and correctly guided intuition of every performer, without which music would remain inoperative. The validity of a musical practice is measured by its efficiency within its own field of application and by its facility to generate the ethos without which it remains ineffectual.[6] Only after mastering this set of criteria can an apprentice musician, of any origin, identify with the substance of a musical tradition, and therefore develop its expressive potential.

It is obvious that, in the present situation, rare are those that achieve this degree of excellence in interpreting music of foreign origin. The investment most genres require is very limiting, sometimes involving degrees of asceticism difficult to reconcile with the pressures of the modern world. Who can dedicate ten years or more exclusively to a discipline of this nature? Initial enthusiasm is often deadened by all kinds of challenges which occur during an apprenticeship. Economic problems, especially those of an uncertain professional future, will at the very least contribute to discourage a student even more; and it is very true that opportunities are rare and, at present, concert organisers generally tend to hire native artists rather than 'converted' ones. Other students come up against impassable psychological barriers:

---

6   This effect of music can almost be of a magical nature if one thinks of the numerous traditional practices of music therapy or the induction of ecstasy and trance through music (see During 1988 and Rouget 1985). The influence of music is not necessarily limited to the human species, since numerous experiments have demonstrated its effects on animals and plants, and various traditions affirm the influence music can have on natural phenomena.

lingering doubts about their real capacities of absorption; difficulties in overcoming the obstacle of mental shock; sensitivities disturbed by the emotional implications of a lasting relationship between master and disciple, with the supposed prerogatives of the one and duties of the other. ...

The way is strewn with traps, in certain respects comparable to the tests that face initiates on a mystical path. Able to discourage the apparently most determined of minds, they sometimes bare the ego, depriving it of the usual references and even proceeding to provoke violent demonstrations of rejection. This set of difficulties equates to a stern selection process that results in there being only a few Westerners completely dedicated to musical practices of this kind who finally become recognised as qualified performers. Some cases, however, inspire a certain optimism; their presence and tangible success are certainly going to play important roles in the evolution of the musical world in general by leading the rest of us towards the acquisition of other musical 'colours'.

Music and cultures 'of the world' are becoming increasingly known and appreciated by many lovers of the arts, and this phenomenon will contribute to the development of other issues related to the provision of this type of artistic training. Acquisition of professional expertise is indeed not the only aim for students of traditional music, that much is obvious Most such students are content with a general sensitising in the principles of a sound aesthetics, either with the intention of integrating some of those elements into their personal styles of expression, or for the simple pleasure of sharing an experience and the artistic and cultural enrichment it offers.

Chapter 11

The Fascination of India
Lessons from Personal Experience

It is an accepted fact today that the eruption of Indian music on the Western musical landscape modified radically our general perception of music. For about half a century the Hindustani musical traditions of northern India – and, on a smaller scale, the Karnatak tradition of southern India – have been revealed in the West in the full dimension of their genius. Indian music had the fortune to become one of the first genres made known to the West through the talent of great ambassadors, including Vilayat Khan, Ravi Shankar, Ali Akbar Khan, Hariprasad Chaurasia, Bhimsen Joshi and Bismillah Khan, to mention masters from the older generation alone.

Thanks to these and so many other artists' unequalled talent we were able to discover the full potential of this expression of inexhaustible resources that rests on three essential concepts, all of which lack equivalents in the European classical tradition: a fundamentally modal melodic structure, the *rāga*; a rhythmic conception of cyclic nature, the *tāla*; and a largely improvised interpretation, destined to expound an ethos, a particular flavour, which Indians call *rasa*. The passage through India was necessary for us to achieve a fuller understanding of the dimension of musicality in its whole diversity of possible applications on a human scale; it has in any case greatly contributed to questioning the West's biased assumption of supremacy in all domains of creation, including the artistic.

I am being careful when isolating India from the other non-Western musical cultures in this respect, and in believing that Indian music alone merits being identified as widening our perception in this regard. It was certainly one of the first to be extensively disclosed to the Western music-lover, and its discovery aroused further desires, often inspiring the music-lover to explore other musical regions or countries, every time more distant and radically different. In fact, as demonstrated in certain studies (Albèra 1996), there is practically no twentieth-century Western composer who has not – whether closely or at a distance – been influenced by his or her own discovery of an extra-European musical tradition.

What was until recently the privilege of a few explorers of unpublished musical worlds has nearly become a fashion nowadays; or in any case a fully fledged cultural trend of considerable dimensions. Almost all so-called traditional music of the world has become accessible to the Western listener, as is proven by the abundance of concerts, festivals, radio broadcasts, discs and all the other means of dissemination offered for their appreciation. The amateur can appreciate the *shash maqām* of Bukhara, the Arabo-Andalusian *nūbāt*, the art of Manding griots or Cuban *soneros*, or even the Pygmy polyphonies of Central Africa or the great pieces for Balinese *gamelan* as easily as the Hindustani *rāga* masters. Listeners can refine personal tastes, make choices based on acquired knowledge, discuss the talents of a genre's different interpreters and appreciate their technique and inspiration with steadily increased discernment. Aficionados of Indian music should never keep this reality out of sight. At a certain stage, our appreciation for the music of India has necessarily driven us – Westerners – to the discovery of other musical cultures, other innumerable musical worlds, permitted us to explore through their diversity the reality of that marvellous and universal talent which is musicality.

An Entry into Tradition

I am personally indebted to the music of India – and there are certainly several of us in this position – for an overture in my musical perception, a radical and definitive overture achieved in particular during long years of practising the *sarod*, a plucked stringed instrument, as well as in several journeys which contributed to my rethinking of my own field of musical perception, my manner of living in music and, to a large extent, my vision of the world itself. Now, it is impossible for me to listen to a genre, whatever it is, as before, my auditory exigency having transformed itself so much. Such an initiation has driven some to dedicate their whole lives to that demanding mistress which is Indian music, and others to use the processes and techniques they encountered on an individual creative path. I was incapable of this – or rather, I did not feel the urgency – and rather my personal aspirations pushed me to apply this teaching, precious above all, to spheres other than mere musical practice.

At the age of 23, academic studies in ethnomusicology and a reasonably nomadic musical life led me on my first journey to the East: a journey of the 'fundamental experience' type which René Daumal described so well (1953: 265–74), a journey with the nature of an initiation, in relation to which there would henceforth be a before and an after, a journey from which one does not come back unscathed. The immersion in the Indian musical environment was to affect my most intimate being to the degree that, for numerous years, I remained incapable of listening to anything but the great masters of Hindustani art, trying hard to follow their traces and, beginner that I was, scrupulously applying the lessons conferred on me by some amongst them.

The more I learned, the more I realised the immensity of my ignorance and the path I had yet to undergo. This inspiring discovery removed from me any wish to consider any existence other than that of docile and determined *shishya* (disciple), accumulating the particularities of what was both a science and an art, something for which I had no equivalent in my previous experience. Little by little, the different sonorous landscapes of each *rāga* took shape, albeit imperfectly, in my conscience and under my fingers. This dream allowed me to escape the contingencies of time and enter a world of new dimensions – for me at least – and of inexhaustible artistic potential.

Soon, the asceticism of apprenticeship was reinforced with a ludic dimension, especially devoted to the discovery of all the rhythmic subtleties of the art; I gained the latter thanks to the complicity of friends studying *tablā* who gladly shared with me a part of their instrumental practice time. Little by little, the music gained shape and life under my fingers; from the obsequious reproduction of taught models I progressed to the stages of gestation, then interpretation and sometimes even inspiration. After they had been ingrained in me thanks to the methodical precepts of *guru-shishya parampara* (master's teaching to a disciple), the *rāgas* acquired their own existence, their distinctive flavours leading me to discover from the inside the masterly consistency of this musical system. There was nothing of a theoretical enquiry in this experience, but rather my fastening onto a properly initiatory tradition, and the progressive realisation of my being's potentiality. Thus, I was brought to understand that, if the cognitive process and 'sound material' at play were Indian, their application surpassed any ethnic or cultural limitations; this music became mine, or rather, I began to identify with it through a kind of alchemical process for which my affinities had revealed the potential.

The famous distinction between nature and culture, innate and acquired, now appeared to me in a striking new way, which is to say that I had formed a new consciousness of the fundamental unity of the human condition. It was now impossible for me to believe in the fable of genetic determination of cultural acquisition; and this I owe above all to the teaching of Indian music, even though today I have abandoned its practice.

The Duck in the Henhouse

One of the questions that comes to the mind, sooner or later, of anyone who dedicates an important part of their time and energy to a discipline as demanding as musical practice concerns the ultimate aim of their study. Apart from the more contemplative of individuals, the desire to share the acquired experience and expertise implies a trajectory open to the possibility of performing in public and, in the longer term, establishing oneself as a professional. In actual practice this is a relatively rare outcome. Indeed, for the 'converted' performer there are all kinds of supplementary difficulties on top of those that worry every would-be musician. The two main handicaps are: first, of a psychological nature, resulting from the acquisition of knowledge from a culture in which the performer was not born; and, second, of a socioeconomic nature, concerning the credibility of the path with respect to others, as much in the eyes of existing holders of such knowledge as in those of a public little or not at all familiarised with the music's performance.

It is true that for a Westerner, an apprenticeship such as that in Indian music places in question most of his or her aesthetic criteria; consciously or not, he or she transforms them radically at the level of deep musical perception. Even though today it is possible to learn to play the *sitār*, *sarangi* or *tabla* in Europe, North America or Japan without even having been to India, such a discipline implies a cultural isolation which, in itself, is practically equivalent to a spiritual asceticism – but is not the practice of music in India considered one of the ways of yoga? The determination of 'displaced' students must be of exceptional firmness insofar as their training is not supported by an auspicious social environment. With only a few exceptions, the diplomas of expertise that they can acquire when the training takes place in an institutionalised organisation will be of no use in their professional future.

The credibility of Western performers of Indian music depends on many other factors, the first evidently being connected to the degree of acquisition of the discipline. If learning has been mediocre, they will not delude listeners for very long. They might possibly impress, or even trick, some unsuspecting audiences or arouse the sympathy of the Indian public – which is sometimes almost overcompassionate towards a well-intentioned foreigner (there is nothing worse on these occasions than to hear a compliment like: 'Not bad for a Westerner!', all the more when it is sincere). But the reactions of experts will soon indicate the actual degree of accomplishment, their approval, in every case, being the only real certification of the musician's achievement.

In any case, the recognition of an artist's talent, acquired outside the context of his or her chosen culture, undergoes a supplementary handicap because his or her trajectory is constantly susceptible to being questioned, even judged as suspicious, by those who perceive only its appearance. The benefits, on the other hand, include the advantage of being a 'duck in the henhouse': a kind of exception that proves the rule, or the hostage of self-righteous minds always anxious to demonstrate the universality – and therefore excellence – of their own music, of their own culture. The first Eastern virtuosos of Western classical music and the first European jazz performers have certainly been through similar experiences.

The Tree and Its Fruit

We know how valorising it is for an Indian musician to have a court of Western disciples. The tree is acknowledged by its fruit: the foreign pupils testify to the master's excellence; they are the signs of his or her prestige and international fame. But – and as sincere as they may be and independently of these questions of prestige – few masters worry about the opportunities that their teaching offers the pupils. Is this their role anyway? It is true that in the long term the most gifted disciples can overshadow or at least offer potential competition to their masters. This is one of the reasons underlying a major principle the teacher always endeavours to instil: not only that of respect, but also of absolute obedience to the *guru*, at least with regard to his area of expertise.

After ten or more years of arduous training, the Westerner who is qualified for a professional career and anxious to jump into it is confronted with an inextricable situation, insofar as he or she still has to learn the mechanisms of the artistic-cultural world and the strategies needed in order to penetrate it. Equally real is the fact that his or her talent must necessarily be matched by a good business sense, unless the performer has inherited a fortune to cover all material needs. The doors of prestigious theatres, large festivals and the all too rare competent artistic agencies in this domain are generally closed, for reasons arising from simple ethnic considerations: he or she does not have the looks for the job; the public will not flock after such a musician. ... The performer's candidature bothers everyone and will often be rejected because the Indian competition is enormous and, among those rare concert promoters open to these genres, even a mediocre Indian will nearly always be preferable because he or she is apparently more believable than a Westerner.

An apprenticeship in Indian music is therefore a lesson in humility, to such an extent that one can wonder if such an artist's life has indeed a purpose. So, what are the other opportunities? The academic profession requires its entrants to have previously followed an academic course of study, and it is certainly a fully valid solution for those with the necessary ambition and qualifications. For others, there remains music teaching per se. These obvious solutions have already been the object of numerous reflections concerning principles and methods, especially during the Teaching World Music conferences held in Amsterdam (1992), Basel (1993) and Rotterdam (1995).[1] Therefore, it appears to me that there is no need to return to that discussion. It is necessary to underline, however, that only affiliation with a prestigious institution guarantees a teacher or researcher feasible economic conditions. In this respect, every applicant finds themselves in the position of being either a precursor or an exception in a marginal situation, whether they wish it or not, especially as the number of available posts will always be lower than the number of suitable candidates.

For a transcultural musician, professional opportunities, when they exist at all, are generally located at the periphery of musical practice; the rare instances of this type of performer succeeding in developing a career as a concert artist will for a long time remain the exception that proves the rule. Personally, after thinking for some time about this possibility, I soon realised that my place was elsewhere. About ten years long, my first Indian experience sensitised me in many aspects to 'the music of the other' for which my schooling in ethnomusicology had vaguely prepared me. This participatory approach transformed the vision I had of the musician's profession, a vision until then imbued with a good dose of juvenile idealism. This experience taught me that music was not only a valuable cultural practice, but also an alchemy of the soul – a discipline with severe exigencies, a continuous inner quest whose results constantly escape those who believe they will be able to seize them. The capacity to move the listener is one of the musician's privileges, but it has its price, and an artist's life is often far from as enviable as it appears. The sacrifice it requires is worth the power of music, an unspeakable and particularly magical power which always surpasses everything we might say or write.

I am not in the habit of speaking of myself, and this is the very first time I have tried to indulge in this kind of exercise. But this opportunity has pushed me to develop certain thoughts and establish a set of balanced reflections on one of my most enriching life experiences. My personal case is of little importance; what is meaningful here is that it is in line with a period of history particularly auspicious for fraternisation and cultural exchange between East and West, North and South. After centuries of misunderstanding and reciprocal incomprehension, we can finally begin to dream of a new frame of mind, founded on listening to the other and on mutual respect. In this respect, if India occupies an essential place in the intercultural debate on music, maybe it is because it proposes a nearly perfect model of synthesis between classicism and modernity, between tradition and creation, between fundamental structures and individual expression. This is a universal model, applicable not only

---

1   See Schippers 1992, and Lieth-Philipp and Gutzwiller 1995.

to the musical domain but to life in general. On this subject, we can recollect the words of Louis Dumont (1980: 3–4):

> the universal can only be attained through the particular characteristics, different in each case, of each type of society. Why should we travel to India if not to try to discover how and in what respects Indian society and civilization, by its very particularity, represents a form of the universal? … If one is prepared to devote all the time necessary to studying … Indian culture, one has a chance, under certain conditions, of in the end transcending it, and of one day finding in it some truth for one's own use.

And, for this, as much else, I remain deeply indebted.

References

Adorno, Theodor W. (1976 [1962]), *Introduction to the Sociology of Music*. Trans E.B. Ashton. New York: Seabury Press.

Albèra, Philippe (1996), 'Les leçons de l'exotisme'. *Cahiers de musiques traditionelles* 9: '*Nouveaux enjeux*'. Geneva: Ateliers d'ethnomusicologie/Georg Editeur: 53–84.

Arom, Simha (1991 [1985]), *African Polyphony and Polyrhythm: Musical Structure and Methodology*. Trans. Martin Thom, Barbara Tuckett and Raymond Boyd. Cambridge: Cambridge University Press.

Aubert, Laurent (1985),'La quête de l'intemporel. Constantin Brăiloiu et les Archives internationals de musique populaire'. *Bulletin Annuel du Musée d'ethnographie de la Ville de Genève* 27: 39–64.

Aubert, Laurent (1991a), *Mondes en musique*. Collective work edited by Laurent Aubert. Geneva: Musée d'ethnographie.

Aubert, Laurent (1991b), *Musiques traditionnelles. Guide du disque*. Geneva: Georg.

Aubert, Laurent (1991c), *The World of Music: Musical Instruments of the Five Continents*. Ivrea: Priuli and Verlucca Editori/Geneva: Musée d'ethnographie.

Aubert, Laurent (2000), *Le monde et son double. Ethnographie: trésors d'un muse rêvé*. Collective work edited by Laurent Aubert. Paris: Adam Biro/Geneva: Musée d'ethnographie.

Aubert, Laurent (2004), *Les feux de la Déesse. Rituels villageois du Kerala (Inde du Sud)*. Collection Anthropologie-Terrains. Lucerne: Editions Payot.

Augé, Marc (1998 [1994]), *A Sense of the Other: The Timeliness and Relevance of Anthropology*. Trans. Amy Jacobs. Stanford: Stanford University Press.

Baily, John (1988), *Music of Afghanistan: Professional Musicians in the City of Herat*. Cambridge Studies in Ethnomusicology. Cambridge: Cambridge University Press.

Baud, Pierre-Alain (1996), 'Nusfarat Fateh Ali Khan: le qawwali au risqué de la modernité'. *Cahiers de musiques traditionnelles 9: 'Nouveaux enjeux'*. Geneva: Ateliers d'ethnomusicologie/Georg Editeur: 259–74.

Baumann, Max Peter (1976), *Musikfolklore und Musikfolklorismus. Eine ethnomusikologishe Untersuchung zum Funktionswandel des Jodels*. Winterthur: Amadeus.

Belmont, Nicole (1986), 'Le Folklore refoulé, ou les seductions de l'archaïsme'. *L'Homme* 36/1–2: 259–68.

Bensignor, François and Frank Tenaille, eds. (1995), *Sans visa. Le guide des musiques de l'espace francophones et du monde*. Paris: Zone franche.

Blacking, John (1973), *How Musical is Man?* Seattle: University of Washington Press.

Bonte, Pierre and Michel Izard, chief eds (1991), *Dictionnaire de l'ethnologie et de l'anthropologie*. 2nd revised edn. Paris: Presses universitaires de France.

Brăiliou, Constantin (1960), 'La vie antérieure', in Roland Manuel, ed.: *Histoire de la musique 1. Encyclopédie de la Pléiade*. Paris: Gallimard: 118–27.

Broughton, Simon, Mark Ellingham and Richard Trillo, eds (1994), *World Music. The Rough Guide*. London: Rough Guides.

Chevalier, Sophie and Mehenna Mahfoufi (1993), *Les practiques musicales au sein des communautés issues de l'immigration. Deux exemples: la communauté portugaise à Paris et dans la region parisienne, la communauté maghrébine à Lyon et dans sa region*. Roneotype. Paris: Société française d'ethnomusicologie.

Coomaraswamy, Ananda K. (1956 [1943]), *Christian and Oriental Philosophy of Art*. New York: Dover.

Crettaz, Bernard and Christine Détraz, eds (1983), *Suisse, mon beau village. Regards sur l'Exposition nationale de 1896*. Geneva: Musée d'ethnographie.

Crossley-Holland, Peter (1964), 'Preservation and Renewal of Traditional Music'. *Journal of the International Folk Music Council* 16: 15–18.

Daly, Ross (1992), *Eurasia: Mitos. Ross Daly & Labyrinth*. CD World Network/ WDR 54.035. Frankfurt: Network Medien GmbH.

Daniélou, Alain (1959), *Traité de musicologie comparée*. Paris: Hermann.

Daumal, René (1953), *Chaques fois que l'aube paraît. Essais et notes*, 1. Paris: Gallimard.

Dehoux, Vincent (1996), 'Feuilles de route'. *Cahiers de musiques traditionnelles* 9: *'Nouveaux enjeux'*. Geneva: Ateliers d'ethnomusicologie/Georg Editeur: 131–46.

Desroches, Monique and Brigitte DesRosiers (1995), 'Notes "sur" le terrain'. *Cahiers de musiques traditionnelles* 8: *'Terrain'*. Geneva: Ateliers d'ethnomusicologie/ Georg Editeur: 27–50.

Dumont, Louis (1980 [1966]), *Homo Hierarchicus: The Caste System and Its Implications*. Complete revised English edn, trans. Mark Sainsbury, Louis Dumont and Basia Gulati. Chicago: University of Chicago Press.

During, Jean (1988), *Musique et extase. L'audition mystique dans la tradition soufre*. Paris: Albin Michel.

During, Jean (1994a), 'L'esthétique comme enjeu de la modernité: le cas des arts et des musiques de l'Islam'. *Cahiers de musiques traditionelles* 7: *'Esthétiques'*. Geneva: Ateliers d'ethnomusicologie/Georg Editeur: 27–50.

During, Jean (1994b), *Quelque chose se passé. Le sens de la tradition dans l'Orient musical*. Lagrasse: Verdier.

Dutertre, Jean-François, ed. (1993), *Musiques d'ici et d'ailleurs. Guide des musiques et danses traditionnelles*. Paris: Centre national d'action musicale.

Eco, Umberto (1984 [1968]), *La structure absent. Introduction à la recherché sémiotique*. Trans. Uccio Esposito-Torrigiani. Paris: Mercure de France.

Ellis, Catherine (1994), 'Powerful Songs: Their Placement in Aboriginal Thought'. *The World of Music* 36/1: 3–20.

Erguner, Kudsi (2000), *La Fontaine de la Séparation. Voyages d'um musicien soufi*. Preface by Jean-Claude Carrièrre. L'Isle-sur-la-Sorgue: Le Bois d'Orion.

Erlmann, Veit (1989), 'A Conversation with Joseph Shabalala of Ladysmith Black Mambaso. Aspects of African Performers' Life Stories'. *The World of Music* 31/1: 31–58.

Feld, Steven (1995), 'From Schizophonia to Schismogenesis: The Discourse and Practice of World Music and World Beat', in George Marcus and Fred R. Myers, eds: *The Traffic in Culture: Refiguring Art and Anthropology*. Berkeley: University of California Press: 96–126.

Feld, Steven (1996), 'Pygmy POP: A Genealogy of Schizophonic Mimesis'. *Yearbook for Traditional Music* 28: 1–35.

Giuriati, Giovanni (1995), 'La voie du gamelan. Entretien avec Ki Mantle Hood'. *Cahiers de musiques traditionnelles* 8: *'Terrains'*. Geneva: Ateliers d'ethomusicologie/Georg Editeur: 193–214.

Goormaghtigh Georges (1990), *L'art du qin. Deux texts d'esthétique musicale chinoise*. Mélanges chinois et bouddhiques 23. Brussels: Institut belge des hautes études chinoises.

Hood, Mantle (1960), 'The Challenge of "Bi-musicality"'. *Ethnomusicology* 4/2: 55–9.

Khaznadar, Chérif and Michel de Lannoy (1995), 'Les trois voies de la musique. Entretien avec Chérif Khaznadar par Michel de Lannoy'. *Internationale de l'Imaginaire*, new series, 4: *'La musique et le monde'*: 37–57.

Leante, Laura (2000), 'Love you to. Un exemple de rencontre entre musique indienne et musique pop dans la production des Beatles'. *Cahiers de musiques traditionnelles* 13: *'Métissages'*. Geneva: Ateliers d'ethomusicologie/Georg Editeur: 103–18.

le Bomin, Sylvie (1998), 'Etre dedans ou être dehors. Entretien avec Jean During'. *Cahiers de musiques traditionnelles* 11: *'Paroles de musicians'*. Geneva: Ateliers d'ethnomusicologie/Georg Editeur: 185–201.

Lecomte, Henri (1992), 'L'avant-dernière tentation de l'Occident'. *Trad Magazine* 20: 28.

Leduc, Jean-Marie (1996), *Le dico des musiques. Musiques occidentals, extra-européennes et world*. Paris: Seuil.

le Quellec, Jean-Loïc, ed. (1993), *L'air du temps. Du romantisme à la world-music*. Collection Modal. Parthenay: FAMDT Editions.

Levin, Theodore (1996), *The Hundred Thousand Fools of God: Musical Travels in Central Asia (and Queens, New York)*. Bloomington: Indiana University Press.

Lieth-Philipp, Margot and Andreas Gutzwiller, eds. (1995), *Teaching Musics of the World: The Second International Symposium*. Basel, 14–17 October 1993. Affalterbach: Philipp Verlag.

Lortat-Jacob, Bernard (1995 [1990]), *Sardinian Chronicles*. Foreword by Michel Leiris. Trans. Teresa Lavender Fagan. Chicago: The University of Chicago Press.

Lortat-Jacob, Bernard (1994), *Musiques en fête. Maroc, Sardaigne, Roumanie*. Collection Hommes et musiques 1. Nanterre: Société d'ethnologie.

Maalouf, Amin (2000 [1998]), *On Identity*. Trans. Barbara Bray. London: Havill Press.

McLuhan, Herbert Marshall (1970), *Guerre et paix dans le village planétaire*. Paris: Robert Laffont.

Martin, Denis-Constant(1996a), 'Que me chantez-vous là? Une sociologie des musiques populaires est-elle possible?', in *Musique et politique. Les répertoires de l'identité,* publié sous la direction d'Alain Darré. Rennes: Presses universitaires PUR: 17–30.

Martin, Denis-Constant (1996b), 'Who's afraid of the big bad world music? [Qui a peur des grandes méchantes musiques du monde?] Désir de l'autre, processus hégémoniques et flux transnationaux mis en musique dans le monde contemporain'. *Cahiers de musiques traditionnelles* 9: '*Nouveaux enjeux*'. Geneva: Ateliers d'ethomusicologie/Georg Editeur: 4–21.

Merriam, Alan P. (1964), *The Anthropology of Music*. Evanston, Ill: Northwestern University Press.

Nattiez, Jean-Jaccques (1990 [1987]), *Music and Discourse: Toward a Semiology of Music*. Trans. Carolyn Abbate. Princeton: Princeton University Press.

Oost, P. J. van (1915), 'La musique chez les Mongols des Urdus'. *Anthropos* 10–11: 358–96.

Pearson, Mike (1996), 'Réflexions sur l'ethnoscénologie'. Trans. Pierre Bois. *Internationale de l'imaginaire*, new series, 5: '*La scène et la terre*': 55–64.

Plato (1974 [1955]), *The Republic*. 2nd edn revised, trans. and with introduction by Desmond Lee. Harmondsworth: Penguin Books.

Renz, Cyrill (1986), 'La danse populaire sur scène', in *Conference internationale d'experts: rapport final. Synthèses et recommandations*. Fribourg: Centre CIOFF: 8–23.

Rouget, Gilbert (1985 [1980]), *Music and Trance: A Theory of the Relations between Music and Possession*. Trans. Brunhilde Biebuycke in collaboration with the author. Chicago: University of Chicago Press.

Sakata, Hiromi Lorraine (1994), 'The Sacred and the Profane: Qawwâlî Represented in the Performances of Nusrat Fateh Ali Khan'. *The World Music* 36/3: 86–99.

Schaeffer, Pierre (1996), *Traité des objets musicaux. Essai interdisciplinaire*. New edition. Paris: Seuil.

Schippers, Huib, ed. (1992), *Teaching World Music. First International Symposium on Education in Non-Western Musics in the West*. Utrecht: Vereniging voor Kunstzinnige Vorming.

Segalen, Victor (1995), *Essai sur l'exotisme, une esthétique du divers*. Fontfroide: Bibliothèque artistique et littéraire/Fata Morgana.

Todorov, Tzvetan (1993 [1989]), *On Human Diversity: Nationalism, Racism, and Exoticism in French Thought*. Trans. Catherine Porter. Cambridge, Mass.: Harvard University Press.

Tran, Van Khê (1976), 'Où en sont les traditions musicales?' *Bulletin du Groupe d'Acoustique Musicale* 84: 1–9.

Zanten, Wim van (1994), 'L'esthétique musicale à Sunda (Java oust)'. *Cahiers de musiques traditionnelles* 7: '*Esthétiques*'. Geneva: Ateliers d'ethomusicologie/ Georg Editeur: 75–93.

Zemp, Hugo (1996), 'The/An Ethnomusicologist and the Record Business'. *Yearbook for Traditional Music* 28: 36–55.

Zemp, Hugo and Tran Quang Hai (1991), 'Recherches expérimentales sur le chant diphonique'. *Cahiers de musiques traditionelles* 4: '*Voix*'. Geneva: Ateliers d'ethnomusicologie/Georg Editeur: 27–68.

Index